# HISTORIC HAUNTS of the SOUTH III

## JAMIE ROUSH PEARCE

### THE FIFTH BOOK IN THE
### *HISTORIC HAUNTS SERIES*

Inquiries should be addressed to:
**Jamie Roush Pearce**
historichaunts@yahoo.com

**BOOKS IN HISTORIC HAUNTS SERIES:**
# Historic Haunts Florida
# Historic Haunts Florida II
# Historic Haunts *of the* South
# Historic Haunts *of the* South II
# Historic Haunts *of the* South III

### Foreward:
In this book I tried to include any and all personal experiences I had at each of the locations I've written about. Unfortunately, ghosts, as I like to say, do not perform on cue. In situations where my personal experiences were limited, I tried to interview people who lived or worked at the locations, past or present. Hours of research, traveling to the different locations, visiting, investigating, touring, and interviewing, all went into writing this book and I loved every moment of it!

### Dedication:
First I want to thank my awesome and amazing hubby Deric for helping me continue to do what I love to do, to write. Without his love and support I would be lost. I love you so much sweetheart, you deserve husband of the year!
<3 xox,
~Jamie

I also want to thank my mother-in-law Paula for helping proof read and get the book ready for print on such a time crunch. Love ya, chickie momma!

My Historic Haunts series would not be possible without the support from the locations, past and present, my Historic Haunts Investigations team, my mom for her support from a VERY early age, and all the readers out there. Thank you so much for helping make my dream possible.
Hauntingly Yours,
~Jamie

### Special Thanks:
**Assistant Investigator:** Gayel Roush

**Editing:** Deric Pearce & Paula Dillon

**Design and Layout:** Deric Pearce
All images unless otherwise credited are provided courtesy of the author
Additional photography provided by and copyright Big Stock

First Printing August 2015

# HISTORIC HAUNTS OF THE SOUTH III

Table of Contents

### ALABAMA
A Tower of Terror .................................................................. 5
Repetitious Spirits at the Rawls ........................................... 8

### ARKANSAS
The Haunted Witches Hollow .............................................. 11
Lights, Camera, Paranormal ................................................ 13

### FLORIDA
The Spirited Little Theatre House ...................................... 15
The Amazing Howey Mansion ............................................. 18
Motion Pictures and Moving Spirits ................................... 22
Ghosts Among the Banyan Trees ........................................ 26
Premium Drinks, Pan Am and the Paranormal .................. 28
Ghosts of the Southernmost Lighthouse ........................... 31
Paranormal Turn-Down Service at the Case Monica ........ 33
Paranormal Patrons at the Jefferson Theatre ................... 37

### GEORGIA
Windsor's Winsome Ghosts ................................................. 38
The Cursed Pillar .................................................................. 40
The Wandering Ghost Ship .................................................. 42
Sailer's Spirits at the Naval Museum .................................. 44
Marshalled Spirits at the Old Hotel .................................... 46
The Haunts of Orange Hall .................................................. 49
St. Simons Ghostly Keeper ................................................... 52

### KENTUCKY
Brown's Spectre in Attendance ........................................... 55

## LOUISIANA
*The Gracious Ghost of Mrs. Baughman* ............................................. 57
*The Gangster's Ghosts: Bonnie & Clyde Still Together* ............... 59
*The Prophetic Voodoo Priestess & The Swamp* ........................... 63
*The Most Haunted Cemetery in the World* ..................................... 66

## NORTH CAROLINA
*Spirits Abound at Barley's Taproom* .................................................. 68
*The Dunhill's Playful Spirits* ................................................................ 70
*The Ghostly Writing's on the Wall: The Pub is Haunted* ................ 73
*The Cora Tree Witch* ............................................................................ 76
*Ghosts of the Lost Colony* .................................................................. 77

## SOUTH CAROLINA
*Revolutionary Spirits of Kings Mountain* ........................................ 81
*Drayton's Haunt the Hall* ..................................................................... 83
*The Friendly and Curious Ghosts of the Lodge Alley* .................. 85
*The Ghosts of Ruins and Riders* ....................................................... 88

## TENNESSEE
*The Ghosts of Chikamauga* ................................................................ 90
*Hurricane Mills: The Haunts of Loretta Lynn's Place* ................... 91

## VIRGINIA
*The Brave Ghosts at the Brafferton* .................................................. 93
*An Amorous Apparition at the Brick House Tavern* ..................... 95
*The Phantom Music of Bruton Parish Church* ............................... 97
*The Ghosts of the Governor's Palace* .............................................. 99
*Washinton's Look-A-Like Ghost?* .................................................... 101
*Lavender Heights Potential Haunts* ............................................... 102
*Washington's Prottective Ghost* ..................................................... 104
*The Poe-tential Ghost of a Master of the Macabre* ..................... 106
*About the Author* ................................................................................ 108

ALABAMA

# A TOWER OF TERROR
## Rocky Hill Castle, Courtland, Alabama

*Rocky Hill Castle circa 1935*
*Photo courtesy of the Wikimedia Commons*

In the early 1800s it was common for couples to move to other areas of the country where better opportunities could provide a better life. James Edmonds Saunders and his wife were one such couple. They moved from their native Georgia to Alabama. Saunders, a successful planter and attorney, was no doubt happy to find a plantation only 4 miles from his father Trevor Saunders. The younger Saunders and his wife bought land to build a bigger plantation in the mid 1820s. They eventually secured a total of 640 acres. Most of the land was centered on the hill that the Saunders house sat upon. The Saunders had originally built a small house to live in, but this house would later be removed to make room for their planned larger and grander

Greek revival and Italian style house.
Saunders and his wife demolished the smaller residence and began building the larger home in 1858. The Civil War would put an end to construction, although by that point the house was largely complete. There were several things that made the house stand out from the other houses in the area.

The first was a large Gothic Revival tower reminiscent of European castles. It contained many chambers and a large winding set of steps. This tower was allegedly where Saunders kept an eye on all his slaves. Here he reportedly imprisoned them and secured them to keep them from getting out under the cover of darkness.

The second item that stood out on the property, was a tunnel rumored to have existed on site. This tunnel connected the Tennessee River to the basement of the mansion. Through these tunnels slaves arrived on the Saunder's property from the ships on the river.

Finally the new house itself with its many splendid rooms and main staircase were impressive. In fact, it contained some of the most elaborate woodwork and plasterwork in the state. Couple this with the Tudor Arch and wall connecting it to the tower and one can easily see why the Rocky Hill residence was dubbed a "castle".

5

# ALABAMA
*Historic Haunts of the South III*

### Rocky Hill During and After the Civil War.

Rocky Hill served as a Confederate hospital during the Civil War. Many soldiers were treated here and several, unfortunately died. Some of these soldiers are buried on the property in the Saunders' Family Cemetery.

After James' death in 1896, the property went through many different owners. In the 1920s Dr. Dudley Saunders, the last Saunders to own it (James' grandson) and his family, abandoned the estate during their ownership, Saunders and his family reported a variety of a paranormal activity that ultimately drove them to leave the house abruptly. Some reports describe a bold and aggressive male spirit who spoke to Mrs. Saunders in her bedroom. The family gathered their things in short order and never came back!

H.D. Bynum and R.E. Tweedy bought the property from Saunders for the farmland and the home/castle began to fall into a state of disrepair. It was rumored that unusual paranormal activity in the house kept the new owners (like the Saunders before them) from permanently residing there. As time passed the mansion rotted and fell to ruin. In 1961, Gordon McBride another new owner salvaged numerous items from the plantation to build his new home in Decatur. Shortly after the McBride's salvaging the house and the tower were demolished. All that is left of Rocky Hill is the vague outline of a foundation beside Highway 72 and some energy that still lingers where it once stood.

### Rocky Hill's Haunts

Even though the building is no longer here, by all reports it seems the land is still holding on to energy from its past and the spirits are still residing there. This isn't uncommon, it actually happens more often that a lot of people realize. Rocky Hill Castle experienced a lot of events that could have caused a lingering ghostly presence of three.

Some believe that Rocky Hill's first ghost was the French architect who had created it. The architect died unpaid for his services and reportedly "hammered" away at the foundations. This phenomenon would continue until the house was leveled! His apparition is still reportedly seen today.

Whether the architect's spirit was the first on site is a matter of some discussion. Some reports state that even Mrs. Saunders thought the place was haunted as far back as the 1820s. She was said to have reported hearing chains rattling and moaning sounds in her home and seeing a woman in a petticoat.

There are also many stories about a "Blue Lady" haunting the property. Her spirit has been seen wandering throughout the area. She has been described as a very sad looking individual with a mournful expression. Her appearance

# ALABAMA
*A Tower of Terror*

seems to bring a gloomy and melancholy air to the regions she's seen in by those who experience her. Her spirit and various encounters with her have been reported as far away as the road heading from the nearby creek to Rocky Hill Castle.

Another account of ghostly activity is that of the apparitions of Civil War soldiers who have been seen on the property. Locals believe the soldier apparitions that are seen are the ones buried on the property. Victims of the Civil War in many cases are not exactly resting in peace.

As if these other accounts and incidents of paranormal activity weren't enough, Rocky Hill also boasts frequent reports of phantom footsteps, disembodied voices, light anomalies, mysterious mists, unexplained knocks and bangs, and general feelings of uneasiness. Many believe these could be the work of the tortured spirits of former slaves from the plantation days.

## A Few Parting Thoughts

This is one location I would have loved to have checked out before the building was leveled. The Revolutionary War and the Civil War are my favorite periods in American history so I try to explore related sites, even on vacations. I hope to get up to Rocky Hill with some of my team and equipment soon to see whether, for these ghosts and others, their home truly is their castle.

# ALABAMA
*Historic Haunts of the South III*
# REPETITIOUS SPIRITS AT THE RAWLS
*Rawls Bed & Breakfast, Enterprise, Alabama*

Enterprise, Alabama is famous, or so some would say. Besides being the only state in the U.S. to erect a large monument to an insect pest (the Boll Weevil monument in the middle of main street); it is also the host of the large music festival "Bama Jam" and the home of Army Aviation (at nearby Fort Rucker). Those who come to see the statue, enjoy the music festival, or learn more about aviation sometimes need a place to stay. One of the most accommodating and hospitable according to locals and many travel sites is the Historic Rawls Bed and Breakfast. As some guests staying at this gracious and beautiful Bed and Breakfast learn; they are not the only ones staying here! The Rawls is known by many to be haunted and has been for quite some time.

## The Rawls Rises

Japheth Rawls, a developer of Coffee County's earliest turpentine plants, and his wife Elizabeth built a small two story structure hotel in 1903 in Enterprise Alabama. When it first opened it was named the McGee Hotel (after its manager). A few years later the name was changed to the Rawls Hotel. It was modeled after a Florida Spanish mission style hotel.

Japheth and his wife wanted the hotel to have its own unique character. To that end they incorporated rare teak in the doors, cherrywood in the stairway railing, and chestnut for the fluted pillars and pilasters. The hotel was a work of art and ran efficiently and smoothly until the time of its founder's death.

Japheth died in 1925 and left the hotel to Margaret Rawls, the wife of his nephew Jesse P. Rawls. They took over the hotel and expanded it in 1928 by adding two three story wings to the main part of the building. In town guests and weary train travelers reveled in the elegant new structure with all its new and unique features.

The Rawls Hotel at one time was the only building in town with heated grates and electric lights. Jesse Rawls was the founder of the first electric power system

# ALABAMA
*Repetitious Spirits at the Rawls*

in Enterprise so he made sure that their hotel had all the electrical amenities. He also saw to it that the hotel became the heart of some of the local social scene by hosting receptions, teas and meetings for several clubs and organizations. The hotels hey-day lasted through the 1940s.

World War II brought trains loaded with passengers, supplies and troops, many on their way to boot camp or seaports. In fact, many published reports claim the train engineers timed their arrivals around noontime so passengers and crew could enjoy the well known lunches served at the Rawls Restaurant (still in operation and still famous for its food). Unfortunately, the hotel ceased operations in the early 1970s.

By the late 1970s the hotel had fallen into disrepair and was sold to Hayden Pursley. He spent three years restoring it to its former elegant glory. The hotel has been listed on the National Register of Historic Places since the 1980s. For all of his efforts, Pursley received a key to the city during the hotel's centennial birthday year in 2003. Pursley passed in 2004. Whether his spirit has joined the others residing at the hotel remains to be seen.

## Supernatural Residents of the Rawls

Tales of the paranormal are nothing new to this Enterprise favorite, reports of paranormal activity have been made since shortly after World War I. However, the paranormal activity seems to have increased as soon as Pursley began his restoration efforts. Pursley stated that during the renovations (and during his time owning the hotel) he frequently saw the apparition of a little girl around the age of 12 running and laughing down the hallway. She always vanished right in front of him. Guests have corroborated these reports.

Apparently there are other children's spirits here as well. Other witnesses have reported hearing children laughing on the third floor and outside of the ladies restroom in the hotel restaurant. These children have also been heard chatting in the basement. The children's apparitions have also reportedly been seen in the basement adorned in 1920s style clothes. They are believed to be residual haunts, and may or may not be responsible for the other unusual activity reported on the 2nd and 3rd floors. Guests and others have reported footsteps, running noises, doors opening and closing, and phantom smells of cigars and perfume even when those floors have been unoccupied.

Cold spots are felt in many locations of the hotel and whispers that can never be made out. Footsteps seem to follow employees and guests down the halls, but when they turn around there is no one there. Kitchen staff have reported that objects in the kitchen are frequently moved. Waitresses claim to have seen Japheth Rawl's apparition in the cellar on more than one occasion. The unusual activity doesn't end there though.

# ALABAMA
*Historic Haunts of the South III*

Many guests of the hotel have described feeling drained of energy when attempting to enter and occupy the ballroom for any lengthy period of time. Disembodied voices and phantom piano music have all been heard coming from this room. An interesting thing to be sure, since as of this writing the ballroom contains no piano!

Whether tickling the ivories or visiting the 2nd and 3rd floors, the spirits at the Rawls seem very active. Visiting fans of the paranormal might find that they are not alone in the main building, grabbing a drink at the bar, or enjoying their meals in the Rawls Restaurant. Regardless, the amazing offerings of this Historic Haunt, like the spirits, require further investigation.

ARKANSAS

# THE HAUNTED WITCHES HOLLOW
Witches Hollow, Cave City, AR

If you want ridiculously good watermelon in Arkansas everyone in the surrounding area knows you have to go to Cave City. Cave City, Arkansas is a small community of roughly 2,000 people in Independence and Sharp Counties. The delicious vine-ripened fruits that bring people to the area and have grown there for years, is something else. A legend has taken seed in Cave City. It grows more year after year drawing those curious about the paranormal, like fans of watermelon. The legend concerns the reports of hauntings at Witches Hollow.

### Which Witch is Which?

The details surrounding the local legend of Witches Hollow are almost as varied as the suggested locations (although all are nearby one another). In several stories, many years ago, a woman was accused of being a witch. Further, it was believed she murdered her husband in his sleep. Variations of this story claim that her husband died of an accident. Regardless of the version of the story, the woman regretted the loss of her husband and heartbroken became a recluse, mourning his death until she too passed away. Her unusual behavior and tendency to come out at night led the townspeople to believe she was a witch. She was accused of witchcraft, but was never tried and there really wasn't any "proof" that she was a witch. Tales of the "witch" and reports of paranormal phenomenon still persist, with another detail that changes like the legend, the actual location!

There are at least 6 different locations in the greater area all reportedly leading to Witches Hollow (and all claimed by locals to be the true way to get to the hollow). Whatever way one takes a dirt or sandy road is the way to get to the old place, and paranormal incidents have reportedly occurred on each, including spectral dancing lights, apparitions and overwhelming feelings of uneasiness. The woman's house in almost all versions is an abandoned place that once may have been part of a village.

### Witchcraft Still in the Works.

The accused witch's home still stands today and many who have been near the abandoned home have become very ill. Many have claimed to have seen spectral lights and other unusual activity. Others have reported seeing a transparent form appearing to be a woman sobbing. The witch's apparition is seen perhaps most frequently on the dirt road(s) leading to her place. While it is

# ARKANSAS
*Historic Haunts of the South III*

certainly possible that all ways do lead to her former residence, and it is not uncommon for a spirit to haunt more than one surrounding location (and in fact she has reportedly been seen on all of these roads); she is most often seen on the path connected to Sandtown Road.

*My Pointed (Hat) Observations.*

I have not been able to get up to Cave City to investigate (or for watermelon for my husband), but hope to soon. This is one of those persistent stories that comes to me frequently and piques my interest (I had two ancestors accused of witchcraft in the Salem witch trials). If I can get up there soon perhaps I can track down the correct location(s) and I might be able to de-mystify those local tales a bit. Regardless the stories of Cave City and the witch have certainly cast a spell on me.

# LIGHTS, CAMERA, PARANORMAL?
## Dover Lights, Dover, Arkansas

Spectral lights are a common "ghost tale" especially in the U.S. and something I have written about before. In my second book, Historic Haunts of the South, I talked about the Brown Mountain Lights in North Carolina. Like the Brown Mountain Lights the Dover Lights (named after the region in Arkansas where the phenomenon occurs) manifest themselves frequently and have done so for generations, but their history and potential background is somewhat unique.

### Reports of Arkansas Lights

Arkansas has a number of unusual and "ghostly" lights including tales of glowing spectral ephemera in Gordon (Clark County) and Crossett. However, visitors and residents of this area of the Ozarks and near Big Piney Creek in particular, have reported this phenomenon for quite some time. Long enough in fact to pre-date electric lights (since the 1800s).

### The Dover Lights Legends

Some people believe the lights are actually the spirits of Spanish Conquistadors searching for lost treasure from hundreds of years ago (many in this region believe Hernando De Soto and his conquistadors made it this far into the state and had contact with the Tula Indians and there is much evidence to back up these claims). Other reports consider the possibility that the Dover lights are from the ghosts of silver miners from the late 1800s still searching for their silver. Those who consider this story claim the spectral lights are from their lanterns. A smaller group of witnesses and locals suspect the lights are UFOs, swamp gas or other unusual natural phenomenon.

### Seeing the Lights

Many people drive along Highway 7 and other areas that look down on to the valley to try and catch the strange phenomenon that appears on a practically nightly basis. Hundreds of reports from witnesses who have seen the lights describe extremely similar activity. Late at night when all is quiet, strange lights appear in the valley glowing many different colors. Many claim the lights respond to sounds and other lights aimed towards them and that the presence of these things may draw them to move closer. Some say if you shout out to the lights they will stop floating or moving around and will fixate on you before starting towards you.

With no roads, utilities or residences situated in the area; the repeated presence of the lights is even more intriguing. So too are some of the eyewitness statements that claim that once the attention of the lights is drawn, they have been known to change colors (typically red, blue, or green) and occasionally to keep pace with vehicles moving through the area. Whether the lights are ghosts, balls of earth's energy, or UFOs, it is a pretty amazing phenomenon and worth investigating for yourself.

FLORIDA

# THE SPIRITED LITTLE THEATRE HOUSE
Athens Theatre, Deland, Florida

*The Athens Theatre*

I admittedly have a soft spot for old movie and theatre houses. When I saw the facade of the fabulous Athens Theatre in Deland, I had to learn more about the place. When I learned that this beautiful landmark was haunted, I had to investigate and put it in a book!

History of the Athens

The Athens Theatre was designed in 1921 by Orlando architect Murray King and developed by L.M. Patterson, a native of Washington D.C. who organized the Deland Moving Picture Company. It is one of the few examples of an American theatre in Central Florida with Italian Renaissance architecture. It opened on January 6th, 1922 and hosted vaudeville acts, silent movies, and live performances. Some have even called it "Florida's handsomest theatre". Besides its memorable productions, attendees were treated to music and sound effects performed on a large Wurlitzer organ.

During the depression, the theatre was the only entertainment people in the Deland area could afford. Over the years it had been more than just a theatre its

15

# FLORIDA
*Historic Haunts of the South III*

been a social center for Deland, serving as a restaurant, dinner theatre, and a video game room. It was renovated in the 1950s, but closed in the early 1990s.

In 1994 with help from the Florida Bureau of Historic Preservation's matching grant, the Main Street Deland Association, bought the theatre for the people of Deland. The Sands Theatre Center Inc. took ownership in 2004. The building has been beautifully restored over the last several years. Now, this grand lady hosts film festivals, concerts, musicals, independent art films, and more. Even ghosts!

## Apparitions at the Athens?

It seems at least some of the spirits attached to the building might come from another structure that once stood where the theatre now stands. At one time before 1921, a livery stood at this location. Two young children named Maria and Isaac lived there with their parents. The brother and sister apparently died of cholera at a very early age and are said to be the ones who haunt the theatre. There have been reports of activity for quite some time.

In January 2015, my team and I set out to investigate the theatre and see if we could make contact with the two youngsters and any other entities present. During our interviews, theatre performer and staff member Alan shared with us some of the paranormal incidents at the Athens and the fact that he himself had seen the little girl's apparition in a long white nightgown or dress.

According to Alan the lights at the theatre have been known to turn themselves on and off as if whoever is there is playing with the staff. The theatre seems to be most active when a production is going on. This perhaps due to the fact there are more people present for the spirits to play with.

Alan also mentioned that the spirits love to get into the cast member's makeup kits and play with the makeup. They also allegedly hide the microphone tape, move things around in the dressing rooms, and stuff things down into the couch in the green room.

There have been a number of paranormal groups that have investigated the Athens, many have reportedly captured activity. These groups have reported instances of strange mists and orb occurrences, as well as occasional EVPS. However, as I looked over more and more current details of investigation teams it seemed so many had investigated that the spirits at the Athens have grown tired of it and provided less and less evidence as of late.

Following what seemed to be the trend, my team (which included my husand and myself as well as Eric and Jolyn O'Dierno) had very little activity. We did not doubt the reports by the other paranormal groups of activity here at the theatre, but we were hoping for our own. We only had a couple of experiences, and one was flash light interaction in the dressing room and the green room. I asked the children if they wanted some chalk to play with and when I said this, the flash light started rapidly turning itself on and off, activity that Jolyn O'Dierno and I both witnessed.

# FLORIDA
*The Spirited Little Theatre House*

My husband Deric and investigator Eric O'Dierno experienced a few unusual spikes in the EMF meter while on the Athen's stage. However, the proximity to the large stage lighting power conduit (and its high EMF readings) are hard to ignore, and shed some doubt on their readings. They could even explain some of the "sightings", as high EMF's have been known to cause many conditions in people including hallucinations. The next time we investigate maybe the spirits will put on more of a show.

Whether you are looking to experience the paranormal at the Athens or not, it is definitely a great place to come for a production. The theatre is an amazing piece of restored theatrical history, and Alan and the rest of the production players lovingly tend to it. No matter where you sit in the theatre, you will have a great view, and you never know, you might even experience a paranormal production yourself.

*NOTE: While researching this story I learned that the theatre has been hosting an annual "Spooktacular" Halloween event for years for Deland's residents. We saw nothing that would indicate they would "stage" or set up incidents to capture on film for paranormal teams. Instead they merely decorate for the occasion and the theatre's haunted reputation helps bring the local crowd. Interestingly enough, however, according to an internet newspaper based in the area, their 2009 event was cancelled due to a series of unfortunate events tied to the "Rosewell Brick". This brick seems to bring misfortune and bad luck to all who display or touch it. Stay tuned for Historic Haunts of the South IV, where I hope to explore this in more detail.*

# FLORIDA
*Historic Haunts of the South III*

# THE AMAZING HOWEY MANSION
*Howey Mansion, Howey-in-the-Hills, Florida*

*Howey Mansion*

Located in Howey-in-the-Hills Florida is an amazing mansion. Designed in the Mediterranean revival style, with a "hostess house" design concept, it may be the only existing example of this kind of structure. Its' known as the Howey Mansion. Unique in its wide lawn, wrought iron entrance gates, and lengthy horseshoe shaped drive, the mansion is something of a legend. Celebrated in its heyday for its beauty and inner detail (curving stone staircase, magnificent fanlight with peacock plumage, pricky cypress woodwork, and massive front door) the mansion is a rare investigative gem in the paranormal investigator's bonnet and an amazing haunted location. A tribute to its creator Mr. Howey.

*William Howey*

### The Story of Howey Mansion

William John Howey was born on January 19th, 1876 in Odin Illinois. He became a successful salesman by the time we was only 16 years old working in insurance and developing lands and towns for the railroad in Oklahoma. In 1903 he opened Howey Automobile Company in Kansas City. His car company made seven Howey cars before he decided to close the business. By the time Howey was 31, he bought land in Mexico and hoped to develop pineapple plantations. Unfortunately, the Mexican Revolution quickly put an end to that endeavor. However, it did leave him with a taste for exploring futures in fruit farming.

# FLORIDA
*The Amazing Howey Mansion*

When Howey moved to Winter Haven Florida, in 1908, he started a citrus farming and sales program technique. He developed a technique in which land was bought for $8-$10 per acre, and sold for $800-$2,000 per acre after it was cleared and planted with as many as 96 citrus trees per acre. Effectively creating on site citrus orchard businesses. Some were not thrilled with this speculative form of business and became enemies of Howey, others jumped at the chance to invest. Howey's ideas made him very wealthy and helped make Florida a citrus growing power.

*Example of the beautiful details in parts of the mansion, here the magnificent fanlight with peacock plumage*

In 1917, Howey built "Bougainvillea", a two story boarding house to house the visiting prospective grove investors. He had amassed nearly 60,000 raw acres and was planning to create a "City Inevitable". Unfortunately, the Bougainvillea burned to the ground in 1920 and he had to set up temporary housing in "Tent City" while he made other plans.

In 1924, he opened the Florida Hotel in "Tent City". It was later featured in Hulk Hogan's "Thunder in Paradise" movie. Released in 1994 the movie featured a sequence in which the hotel was blown up and caught on camera.

Howey completed construction on his mansion on the second site in 1927 (the first site chosen became Bok Tower). It consisted of 20 rooms and 7,200 square feet at the cost of $250,000. To celebrate he hosted the entire New York Civic Opera Company (100 artists) and drew a then unheard of crowd of 15,000 for the free outdoor performance.

The Florida land boom collapsed in 1926, the stock market crash in 1929, and the Great Depression of 1930 put a virtual end to Howey's innovative citrus land sales. He tried unsuccessfully to run for governor. The other ideas in the works for this innovator were never realized.

Howey died on June 7th, 1938 at the age of 62 from a heart attack or so they say. Many believe Mr. Howey was actually murdered, possibly poisoned to death. His wife Mary Grace Hastings lived in the Howey Mansion until her death in December of 1981.

William, Mary, and their daughter Lois are all buried in the family mausoleum on the property. A fifteen acre area called "The Park" because of the variety of botanical plants and local shrubbery. The Howey's have one surviving daughter who lives in Eustis in a nursing home and is now in her 90s.

Howey's Mansion is an extremely beautiful and well known building listed in the National Register of Historic Places. Unfortunately, it has fallen on had times and efforts to revitalize this historic structure and create a venue for a possible

# FLORIDA
*Historic Haunts of the South III*

Inn, wedding destination, and historic tour site are in the works. It is my hope that good folks like Jacklyn Cheatham with the William Howey Mansion community Restoration Project, and Steampunk style paranormal investigator "Colonel Nigel Pennington" might be able to breathe new life into this Historic Haunt.

## Speaking of Historic Haunt

Howey's Mansion resembles a beautiful, but possibly haunted structure. It has taken on an almost legendary status in the Florida paranormal community, few have been inside and fewer have been invited to investigate. I had the opportunity to conduct a day time mini investigation thanks to our friend, Colonel Nigel Pennington who has filmed several of his steampunk adventures here and has his office inside Howey Mansion. He has also investigated the mansion several times himself and had a variety of paranormal experiences.

We took base readings throughout the mansion and the property which rarely fluctuated. The EMF throughout was flat at 0 and the temperature only rose or fell at most .5 of a degree. We also captured little to nothing in the way of EVPs.

As many of you know, just because we visit or investigate a haunted location doesn't mean we will experience anything exciting or paranormal. We didn't see any apparitions or hear any voices while investigating, but I did pick up on a few strange incidents. I developed a sharp pain on the right side of my head at the gate where the driveway leads back to the carriage house/garage. All three times I approached that same area of the gate I got the same pain. When I stepped away from it, it went away. It almost felt as if something unpleasant happened here or as if a ghost was here and didn't like me poking around.

While in the ballroom I was asked to walk around the room to get a feel for the place and see if I sensed anything. Near the steps leading into the front entryway I got slightly lightheaded. I was later told that a medium did a table tipping session some time ago in that very spot and the table actually spun. The smell of something dead arose after the session and it took months to go away. We jokingly speculated that it could have been a dead rat underneath the floor or something conjured up during the session?

When I walked into the bathroom in his office I wondered if Mr. Howey had been poisoned. Even though he died elsewhere and not in his home there was still such a strong vibe. When I went into his personal bathroom I felt very nauseated and light headed. Perhaps he was trying to tell me he had been poisoned. Possibly by someone who stood to inherit something or someone who was jealous of Mr. Howey's success.

While I try to rely on my equipment, sometimes I get sensations about a place that often prove true. When those sensations come on strong, I try to go with them. They were definitely strong in the Howey Mansion.

I also sensed a female presence in the house and I believe it to be Mrs. Howey.

# FLORIDA
*The Amazing Howey Mansion*

It was as if she was still welcoming friends into her beautiful home for another grand gathering. The place was so beautiful I could see why anyone would want to gather there.

This mansion is amazing and is a huge piece of Howey-in-the-Hills history. Jacklynn Cheatham, a resourceful woman is currently in the process of trying to purchase, save, and restore the property and return it to its grand state. If you are interested in helping with a donation, volunteering, etc. please contact Jacklynn through **https://www.facebook.com/HoweyMansion?fref=ts**

If you are interested in seeing some of the fun adventures of Colonel Nigel Pennington and a great deal of Howey Mansion then check out **http://www.thesteampunkempire.com/**

This mansion is truly a beautiful piece of history that we can't afford to lose. I encourage my readers to help in any way they can. As Dr. W.A.R. Goodwin of Colonial Williamsburg once said about preservation "So the future may learn from the past."

*The Howey Family Mausoleum in "The Park"*

## FLORIDA
*Historic Haunts of the South III*

# MOTION PICTURES AND MOVING SPIRITS
*Norman Studios, Jacksonville, Florida*

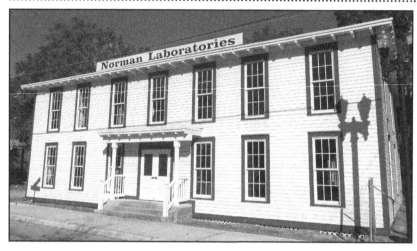

*Norman Studios*

In the early 1900s Florida was the Hollywood of the south and enjoyed a "Gilded Age" as a winter playground for the wealthy. It was too cold to film in cities like Chicago or New York, so Jacksonville became a great location for movies. Earning the title "Winter Film Capital of the World", Jacksonville was aided by a climate that didn't dismay starlets or damage film stock. The addition of the New York-to-Florida rail track made it easy for the well-to-do to come down from the Big Apple. In 1916 there were over 30 motion picture companies in Florida and many were located in Jacksonville.

### The Winter Film Capital of the World

In 1916, Eagle Filming Studios (originally built as a cigar factory) consisted of five buildings in the heart of the Arlington district. The location even had a pool for filming water scenes. That same year a full length film titled "The Green Eyed Monster" was released by Richard Norman. Norman had been born in Middleburg, Florida in 1891 and had strong ties to Jacksonville. He began making movies for white audiences in the 1910's. Among Norman's early ventures was a turn at making "townies", local films produced with local talent in the towns where he traveled. He would screen these for a packed theatre of people eager to see themselves and their friends on the silver screen. Eagle Film Manufacturing would declare bankruptcy in 1917.

# FLORIDA
*Motion Pictures and Moving Spirits*

 Richard and Gloria Norman bought the studio and changed the name to Norman Studios in the early 1920s. Specializing in motion pictures, and "talking picture equipment". The Norman Studios property became known for their powerful films featuring a string of starring black actors. Norman Film Manufacturing Company (also on property) became known in its own right as one of the most sophisticated production film company facilities in the early days of motion pictures.

The Normans, both white, hated the race issues of the time and wanted the black community to have a strong place in the film industry. They made several silent movies starring African American characters in positive, non-stereotypical roles from 1920-1928 and many were filmed at Norman Studios. In 1922 "The Crimson Skull" and in 1926 "The Flying Ace" were filmed here and both became very popular films (the Flying Ace became his most celebrated film and has been restored and housed at the Library of Congress).

Among Norman Studios more notable actors were celebrated individuals like Bill Pickett, America's first black cowboy movie star. He is fondly remembered as the greatest cowboy of the day. Another, Anita Bush a well known Vaudeville and Broadway actress considered by many as the "Mother of Drama in New York Among Colored People". Also, Kathryn Boyd, who starred in the Flying Ace in honor of groundbreaking black female aviator Bessie Coleman. This film would later be seen by young men who would grow up to be Tuskegee airmen.

Besides having an eye for talent and film making, Norman was an inventor. He invested a small fortune into developing a way to sync sound and video, effectively creating motion pictures with sound or "talkies". Unfortunately, before he could sell more than a dozen units, someone else discovered a way to put sound on tape, which effectively rendered his system obsolete. Norman shifted gears, concentrating his efforts on the distribution of other filmmaker's works and on the production

*Two of Norman Studios most famous movies. Courtesy of Norman Studios*

# FLORIDA
*Historic Haunts of the South III*

of corporate training and promotional films (including Pure Oil Company and Joe Louis fight films).

Ultimately, the Jacksonville film industry left after some bad filming incidents. An ultra-conservative, anti-film company mayor was elected and legal wrangling over Thomas Edison film equipment patents. Again, Los Angeles helped expedite the process with their strong efforts and investments to bring the industry to California. Hollywoodland, as it was originally known, would become the new home for motion pictures (it was later shortened to Hollywood).

After the film industry and producers headed west, and Norman retired in 1952, Norman Studios became known as the Gloria Norman Dance Studio (operated by Norman's beautiful and fiery-spirited wife). Her studio was a staple in the community for years, but would eventually close in the mid 1970s. Over time the buildings that made up Norman Studios were emptied out and all closed down.

Ann Burt discovered the old buildings in a state of disrepair and embarked on a long journey to preserve and share her neighborhood's amazing film history. Through a variety of campaigns, nonprofit corporations, and the passionate pursuit of her and her helpers, people took notice. The city of Jacksonville officials stepped up to help along with state and national officials. Four of the five buildings were purchased in 2002, and by 2007 had undergone structural repairs and extensive renovations, returning the buildings to a semblance of their glory days. Efforts continue to be made including the potential purchase of the fifth building, film screenings, capital campaigns, historical presentations, tours of the property and other outreach efforts. All of this to make sure Richard Norman's and Northeast Florida's contributions to cinema history are remembered. Today Norman Studios, a 501c3, is on the National Register of Historic Places and continues to gain attention as the Norman Studios Silent Film Museum, and is Jacksonville's only surviving Silent Film Studio Complex. Many of its props, photos and set pieces are on display at the Museum of Science and History while the site undergoes renovations.

## Learning of Norman Studios and their Potential Haunts

My husband and I stumbled across early references to Norman Studios while researching other stories. We are both old movie fans and as such we looked into it further. After making contact with representatives from the nonprofit groups working to renovate and repair the studios, I learned that there had been some "incidents" on property. These incidents to some suggested the place could be haunted. Among those mentioned were incidents involving mysterious sounds, disembodied voices and the like (activity perhaps brought on by the renovations). This stirred my interest further. I connected with the good folks behind Norman Studios and was graciously told I would be allowed to tour the site with a guide.

  In 2012 I was able to tour the entire property I was very curious about the history. It had such a great vibe to it and there was a good energy flowing throughout the property. I recorded the audio of the tour and took many photos. When I returned home and looked over all the photos and listened to the audio I came across a couple of interesting things. In the audio recording from the tour, I kept hearing disembodied footsteps that traveled with us. It was just a volunteer and myself, no one else was anywhere on the property. Every time we stopped, it stopped in short order. The recording device I was using has no recording delay, so there could be no obvious explanation for the footsteps. Further, the footsteps occurred throughout the entire tour, not just once or twice, and the rooms we toured had no obvious echoes, nor did the footstep patterns match ours. I began to wonder if the spirit of a former worker or actor could have been following us around hearing the guide tell stories about them?

  I tried to arrange a second tour of Norman Studios, but was unable to make the connection due to scheduling and other conflicts and commitments. However, my husband and I returned and did walk the perimeter just beyond the property fence line with more equipment. Our EVP devices once again captured the sound of disembodied and pursuing footsteps. Whoever or whatever may be here certainly seemed to like walking the grounds! My husband and I searched the surrounding areas in an effort to come up with a possible explanation for the footstep sounds, but found none.

  I haven't been able to get back to Norman Studios for a more thorough investigation, but I have been following their efforts including touring their display at the Jacksonville Museum of Science and History during the renovations. Another of my Historic Haunts subjects "the Maple Leaf" (Historic Haunts of the South), has a display practically next door, an interesting coincidence for me. I've decided even if this location wasn't haunted by spirits, it is haunted by some amazing Jacksonville, film industry, and African American history. I am excited that so many are making efforts to preserve it and draw attention to it. It was my intention to include it in an upcoming book to help draw attention to it as well, if I succeed in some small fashion or can move some paranormal fans to look into it further then I will be happy. We have to preserve the past so the future may learn from it.

## FLORIDA
*Historic Haunts of the South III*

# GHOSTS AMONG THE BANYAN TREES
## The Banyan Resort, Key West, Florida

*The Banyan Office*

Tucked away on a Historic Caribbean Estate in the heart of Old Town Key West is the amazing and aptly named Banyan Resort. The Banyan consists of six homes constructed as private residences during the mid 1800s and all surrounded by beautiful and huge banyan trees. The interests of the individual owners were pooled along with an added town house and former Cigar Factory. Together this group makes up the Banyan.

This certified Green Lodge would be enough of a draw for any visitor to the keys with its abundant hospitality, temperature controlled swimming pools, hot tubs, lush and fragrant gardens, and rooftop views. Also in its favor is its close proximity to Duval Street and Mallory Square. Add in the fact that several of its buildings have more than their fair share of ghost stories and you'll understand why I was eager to investigate myself.

### Tales of the Cosgrove House

The Cosgrove House was built in 1850 by a man named Lord and changed hands several times before later being purchased by Captain Phillip L. Cosgrove and his wife Myrtle for $1600 in 1871. He passed the house on to his son. It was passed in time to his granddaughter and it remained in the family until 1947. The two Banyan trees that the Captain's wife planted are still there today. Several stories of the paranormal - like the Banyan trees - have taken root.

The main ghost stories attached to the Cosgrove House that I discovered seemed to center greatly around Room #405. The attic apartment here was thought to be the children's playroom back in the day. Many guests have reported a young child's ghost attempting to get in bed with them during the night. The child appears to be between to ages of 3 and 5. However, some believe there are two children's ghosts here. The other is a little girl said to be looking for her parents which she has been doing for the past 40 years. There are also reports at the Cosgrove House describing several men in late 1800s garb singing and walking down a stair case that is no longer there. The ghost of the Captain himself has been seen here on multiple occasions.

### Details of the Delaney

Also, at the Banyan Resort is the Delaney House (also known as the

Delaney/Sanderson House). It is a Princess Anne style house and it appears on the records as early as the late 1800s when Charles Winfred Sanderson and his wife Lorena Alexandria Harrison lived there. While residing there, he was a part of the 5th Ohio volunteer Infantry Regiment. He was about to depart with his unit for Cuba for the Spanish American War of 1898, but the war ended before he received his orders.

Lorena's father was Reverend Eugene Amelins Harrison of the Old Stone Methodist Church on Eaton Street. When Lorena and Charles married in 1907, they rented the 2nd floor of the house from Mr. William Delaney who is said to have built the house in 1898. They had three daughters and they moved from the home in 1925.

The paranormal encounters at the Delaney House seem to revolve around Room #507 where a female apparition is often seen in the loft area. She also tries to lie in bed when someone is already there and startles the guests. Once they wake up she gets up and walks down the spiral staircase and exits through a wall. Witnesses who have seen her say she appears to be in her mid twenties with long brown hair dressed in early 1900s attire.

## Investigating the Banyan

In April 2015, I had the opportunity to conduct a two night investigation at the Banyan. We were originally scheduled to be placed in one of the more paranormally active rooms, but instead we were given a room in a less active building. Since others were staying in those rooms and we had no wish to disturb them, we limited our investigations to our room and the grounds. My husband Deric and I explored the property getting base EMF and temperature readings. For the most part the EMF stayed level with only slight fluctuations and the temperature was steady around 80 to 82 degrees (which was the air temperature outside).

While exploring the garden area walking under the Banyan trees we experienced the very strong smell of vanilla tobacco and the temperature and EMF dropped significantly, but for only a brief second. When the readings went back to normal, the phantom smell was gone. There was no one else in the garden area with us.

My good friend, author, and fellow paranormal investigator David Sloan has captured EVPs in this area as well with significant temperature drops and EMF spikes. David claims that the trees often serve as a paranormal playground. To back his claim up he has frequently captured the sounds of children's spirits gathering and playing among the trees and experienced them with guests on his tours.

When we retired to our room (#303) after researching the Banyan, its trees and its ghost stories, we really didn't hear too many tales told about our 2nd floor suite. At midnight, however, we heard someone running across the roof. When we checked, there was no one there and apparently no way for them to have gotten up there.

## Final Thoughts

There are so many ghost stories associated with the Banyan (including more detailed encounters of Captain Cosgrove's ghost and others) that it is a fixture on all the local ghost tours. If you want to hear more about the paranormal activities at the Banyan Resort, make sure you check out Sloan's Ghost Hunt.
**www.keywestghosthunt.com**

## FLORIDA
*Historic Haunts of the South III*

# PREMIUM DRINKS, PAN AM, AND THE PARANORMAL

*Kelly's Caribbean Bar, Grill, and Brewery, Key West, Florida*

*Kelly's Sign*

Key West - the Southernmost point of the U.S., is an extremely popular tourist destination in the Sunshine State. While many of these visitors get understandably caught up in glorious sunsets and mile marker pictures; those who dig a little deeper will discover a few wonderful gems off the beaten path. One of these is Kelly's Caribbean Bar, Grill and Brewery. Visitors to this local landmark can soak up the Key West atmosphere under the Banyan trees and learn why the place boasts a strong aviation theme. They may even discover more spirits here than those found behind the bar.

### The Birthplace of Pan Am

A large sign outside of Kelly's proudly recognizes the structure as the birthplace of Pan American World Airways. The Bar, Grill, and Brewery was the first office of Pan American Airways (Pan Am). When it was originally built it was located on the beach. Several years ago it was moved to its current location on the corner of Whitehead Street and Caroline. On October 28, 1927 Pan American Flight No. 1 taxied down the runway in Key West bound for Havana. This was the first United States International Air Service in scheduled operation.

Pan Am was founded originally in response to the encroaching presence of a German-owned Columbian air carrier SCADTA. SCADTA, the world's second airline and first in the "Americas", was seeking landing routes to the Panama Canal Zone, and from there routes for connection to the U.S. The United States Army Air Corps were concerned this upstart company could present a possible German aerial threat to not only the Panama Canal, but the U.S. as well. To make sure SCADTA would never reach this potentially dangerous destiny, the U.S. Government helped insulate the

# FLORIDA
*Premium Drinks, Pan Am, and the Paranormal*

*Pan Am's "Brazilian Clipper"*

fledgling company and protect it from its competition. They also quickly approved delivery contracts and air routes. With this kind of help its no wonder Juan Trippe, Pan Am's early operational head extended routes and reach from Cuba to other parts of the world. At one time he even toured Latin America with Charles Lindbergh to negotiate landing rights.

## Pan Am's Rise and Fall

Pan Am may have started out as a passenger and air mail service with its early seaplanes ("flying boats") operating between Key West and Havana, but it would expand into Miami, North America, Latin America, Europe, and other parts of the world. At its zenith it was the largest international air carrier in the U.S. from 1927 until its demise in 1991. It became a 20th century icon, its blue globe logo known all over the world, and the use of "clipper" in aircraft names and call signs as instantly recognizable as the stewardesses and the white pilot uniform caps. Pan Am is credited with introducing a number of innovations to the airline industry, including the widespread use of computerized reservation systems, jet aircraft, and jumbo jets in particular.

## The Former Pan Am Office Reserves the Right to Brag a Bit

Kelly's is owned and named after movie actress Kelly McGillis, star of Witness, The Accused, and coincidentally Top Gun. In fact, her Top Gun aviators jacket can be found in the "Crash Bar" area. It's no wonder then that the place has details like pop riveted areas to emulate early airplane wings and many other "aerial" influences. If that wasn't enough it was voted one of the 10 Best Key West Restaurants for Outdoor Dining, and Happy Hour by USA Today. It's also the "Southernmost" and premiere microbrewery in Key West and an ideal place to enjoy a layover and a connecting "flight" of craft beers. One last thing I failed to mention, according to my investigations, and those of my good friend David Sloan (who runs a ghost tour in town that launches from Kelly's) the place is haunted!

*Early Pan Am Ad*

# FLORIDA
*Historic Haunts of the South III*

## Kelly's Spirits are Free to Move About the Cabin

Apparently one of Pan Am's past employees is in a holding pattern and never left the office, even after her death and the building being relocated. Her apparition and presence has been experienced by many, especially children. The children dining at Kelly's (and some adults) will ask who the strange woman is and why she is wearing strange clothes. The children's accounts will inevitably match a woman in an old style Pan Am uniform. One of the chefs at Kelly's has nicknamed the female apparition "The Supervisor" because he feels her watching him open up in the mornings. He has told people "I might be the only one on the schedule, but I'm definitely never alone." By all accounts this entity never tries to harm anyone; she just seems to be making sure the work gets done.

A former Pan Am employee doesn't seem to be the only spirit at Kelly's. There seems to be another group of spirits here, from the Victorian era. David Sloan, owner of Sloan's Ghost Hunt, shared a story of a woman who witnessed a group of people in Victorian garb in the garden area of Kelly's. She thought a commercial or television show was being filmed when she saw them. She later asked a staff member at the restaurant who they were, but when the employee looked there was no one there. The employee informed the woman she was the first customer of the day.

## On Final Approach

If you want to hear more details and reports about the spirits at Kelly's, consider joining Sloan's Ghost Hunt. David has investigated Kelly's many times and can tell you in much greater detail the evidence he's collected and the encounters that have been experienced here. Further, David has published several books on the ghosts of Key West. I like to think of him as my Key West connection, a paranormal expert on the haunts of this town, and a good friend for over ten years. I think he'd agree that Kelly's is a must on the itinerary for any Key West visit. If you're a paranormal enthusiast I recommend you grab a cold one, enjoy the shade of the canopy trees in the courtyard and secure one of David's books for your carry on. Then wait to meet at the gate and climb aboard his tour. It's the best paranormal experience in town and David's a great co-pilot!

# GHOSTS OF THE SOUTHERNMOST LIGHT HOUSE
Key West Lighthouse,
Key West, Florida

*Key West Lighthouse*

The first lighthouse located in Key West was a 65 foot tower completed in 1825. It's first keeper was Michael Mabrity. When he passed in 1832, his widow, Barbara became the new keeper and served for 32 years. In 1846, the Great Havana Hurricane destroyed the lighthouse killing 14 people who sought refuge in the tower (including some of Mrs. Mabrity's family). She was spared. Nearby the Sand Key lighthouse was also destroyed. A boat called the Honey was outfitted as a lightship and served faithfully until a new lighthouse could be built.

Completed in 1848, the new tower was 50 feet tall and stood on ground about 15 feet above sea level. Through the years many upgrades and changes were made to the light. These included an extension so it would be seen further out at sea and eventually a third order Fresnel lens was installed (1855).

Mrs. Mabrity was replaced as lighthouse keeper in the 1860s at the age of 82 after discouraging remarks were made by her against the Union. A hurricane hit in 1866 and after damaging the light, led to the replacement of the lantern in 1873 and the addition of three feet to the tower height. The growth of trees and taller buildings began to obscure the light so it was raised twenty feet, putting the light one hundred feet above sea level (1894).

Eventually the light was automated. In 1969 the U.S. Coast Guard decommissioned the tower due to advances in technology. The need for a keeper was gone. The Coast Guard turned the building over to Monroe County who turned it into the Key West Arts and Historical Society.

The light is still lit today and operates as the Key West Light House and Keepers Quarters Museum. On its property is a wonderful museum of its history and the maritime era. It is also said to house several spirits. During my first trip here in 2004, I became aware of its haunted nature and this was before I'd ever heard any paranormal reports about this location.

## My Experiences at the Lighthouse

I believe I came in contact with the spirit of Barbara Mabrity, the once keeper of

# FLORIDA
*Historic Haunts of the South III*

this lighthouse. While touring the grounds on my first trip I was thinking out loud to myself how amazing it was that a woman was the first keeper and how proud I was of this. I began to smell what I can only describe as rose water or an "old-timey" ladies perfume. I quickly walked through the keeper's house and realized I was completely alone.

Later, while climbing the tower I heard footsteps following me up to the top. The way this tower is built, you can look below you and clearly see if anyone is there. I looked down, the footsteps stopped, and I saw no one. When I got to the top, I thought I would see someone and that the footsteps I heard earlier had actually been above me. I got to the top and went outside and there was no one to be seen. After I climbed back down, I went into the gift shop and asked if there were a lot of people touring the grounds. I was informed I was the only one there.

## Key Details on the Lighthouse Ghosts

Mabrity's ghost has been reported often, and may be a residual haunt as she has been seen walking the 88 steps of the lighthouse each night to make sure all is well. Mabrity's spirit is not alone. Dozens of other ghosts have been reported on the lighthouse grounds. There have been other reports describing two Victorian women walking hand in hand and a soldier on the property as well. Further, another two spirits attached to the keeper's quarters reportedly died here from typhoid fever while they worked for the lighthouse.

There are many other haunted locations here on Whitehead Street near the lighthouse including; Ernest Hemingway's House (featured in my first book Historic Haunts Florida and which you can see from the lighthouse) among others. My good friend and fellow paranormal investigator and author, David Sloan, has suggested that Key West's unusually high paranormal activity may be due to its limestone foundation or properties of the surrounding waters (thought by many to attract and hold paranormal energies). I have to agree with him as there are an unusually high number of haunted locations in the area. For more details on some of those Historic Haunts I recommend you pick up David's book Ghosts of Key West. He is the pre-eminent authority on the paranormal in that area and a great writer to boot.

# PARANORMAL TURN-DOWN SERVICE AT THE CASA MONICA HOTEL

Casa Monica Hotel, St. Augustine, Florida

The Casa Monica Hotel opened in 1888 and was built by Franklin W. Smith. It was constructed just across the street from Henry Flagler's Hotel Alcazar (now the Lightner Museum) and Flagler's Ponce de Leon Hotel (now Flagler College), see Historic Haunts of Florida. Smith was a notable Victorian architect and had convinced Flagler to invest in the state of Florida.

*The Casa Monica*

According to many accounts Flagler was not thrilled about having competition directly across from his hotels. Predictably, Smith had problems opening his hotel on time or fully equipped, since he had to rely on Flagler's Railroad to deliver supplies and furnishings.

Soon after Smith's hotel opened he ran into financial difficulties. He sold the hotel and its contents for $325,000 to Flagler. Flagler renamed the hotel the Cordova. Coincidentally, Flagler had no trouble at all getting the hotel fully equipped and opened on time, Flagler welcomed hundreds of guests without any issues.

In 1902 a walking bridge was constructed from the Cordova Hotel to the Hotel Alcazar. The hotel was renamed the Alcazar Annex. Connected portions of the hotel were closed in 1932 due to the great depression. The bridge was removed in 1945.

In February of 1962, the St. Johns County Commission purchased the hotel for $250,000 to use it as the St. Johns County Courthouse. Renovations on the former hotel would take six years, but in the meantime, the building came into the national spotlight. In 1964, the lobby of the vacant hotel housed police dogs that were used against demonstrators in the Civil Rights event involving Dr. Martin Luther King and Dr. Robert Hayling. This demonstration led directly to the passing of the Civil Rights Acts of 1964.

The famous travel agency "Ask Mr. Foster" was once headquartered in the building, and after becoming a national business, was later owned by Peter Ueberroth, the one time commissioner of baseball. The building served as the County Courthouse until the 1990s. It also housed government offices and archives.

In February 1997, Richard Kessler bought the building for $1.2 million. Kessler and his architect did a beautiful job restoring the building to its original Moorish Revival appearance. The building reopened in December 1999 as the Casa Monica Hotel. Since the reopening it has welcomed Archbishop Desmond Tutu, and the King and Queen of Spain. Conde' Nast has rated it one of the Top 20 hotels in Florida, and it is the only hotel in St. Augustine to have been given AAAs four-diamond rating.

## Paranormal Incidents at the Hotel

Stories of the paranormal have been reported here for decades (if I was going to haunt a location, this would be a beautiful one to haunt). Before moving to St. Augustine, I had stayed at the Casa Monica numerous times and it has always been a very special place for me, full of strong and positive energy. I have heard a few of these stories and had a few experiences myself.

During one stay at the hotel, our room was located on the 5th floor and was located in the corner with a view of the pool. I pulled the curtains wide open and my family and I decided to change and go for a swim. As we were in the pool, we looked up at the building and pointed out our room and noticed something. There was a woman in Victorian clothing looking out our window. We looked at each other and realized we were both seeing the same thing.

I quickly got out and grabbed the room key, towel, and shoes and headed straight for the room. I told my mom not to take her eyes off that window until I get up there. As I got to our room door there was a major cold spot as I opened the door. Not as if I was experiencing a blast of cold air conditioned air, but much colder. I opened the door, saw no one and went straight for the window. My mom was looking up at the window and had a puzzled and shocked look on her face. I was like "What happened?" I motioned for her to come up to the room and she did. When she got there I asked her what had happened and she informed me that the woman was at the window just seconds before I got there. The room was completely empty and there was nowhere for anyone to have vanished.

On another occasion I saw a woman in Victorian garb in the ladies restroom off of the lobby. I saw her in my peripheral vision and was going to discuss her fine clothes. When I turned to comment on her attire she was gone.

A dear friend of mine, Megan Morin, worked at the hotel years ago and had a few of her own experiences.

*"I worked as a "Turn-Down Attendant" for the Casa Monica hotel. This meant that we would come in the rooms in the evening and tidy up, throw away garbage, change sheets, soaps and shampoos, fold the bed a certain way and leave a newsletter and chocolate on the bed. Every night the routine was the same, each room a little different. Each employee was given about 2 floors to complete each night. One thing was for sure though. None of the*

# FLORIDA

*Paranormal Turn-Down Service at the Casa Monica Hotel*

*Turn-Down Attendants (as well as House Keepers from what I was told) liked doing one particular floor...the 4th. One night I was talked in to switching floors with another employee who absolutely did not wish to do the 4th floor this particular night. I looked at my checklist after turning down several rooms and noticed the St. Francis suite was next. This is a beautiful 2-story suite with beds downstairs and a Master bedroom upstairs, as well as a sun room in the back. Immediately when you walk in you see a bathroom to your right and then 2 beds on the left. Directly in front of you is a staircase that leads straight up to the Master Bedroom area. As a Turn-Down Attendant you are required to first knock on the door several times waiting for a response before you can enter. Once you enter the room you must still call out, "Turn Down Service!", so that anyone who may have not heard you knocking will hear that you have entered the room.*

    *So I did this normal routine entering the St. Francis Suite and heard no reply. I started to clean the first bathroom downstairs and stopped for a moment because I thought I heard something. Silence. I went back to cleaning and heard something again. This time it sounded like footsteps walking on the floor coming from upstairs. From the bottom of the stairs I called out, "Turn-Down Service!" Silence. "Hello!? Is anyone upstairs?" Footsteps again. "Would you like Turn-Down Service?" Silence. I started walking up the stairs slowly. "Hello? Is someone here?" Now, you may be asking yourself at this point why I would continue going upstairs if someone were in fact there. It would seem logical to leave the suite allowing the guests their personal space, as they clearly were not hearing me or just not responding.*

    *Well for 1.) The Casa Monica Hotel is very strict about cleanliness and upholding the services they offer. Therefore, I could NOT leave a room without providing the service unless specifically asked not to by the hotel guest. The hotel will even do checks or send in their own type of "secret shoppers" to make sure you are doing your job and now 2.) My curiosity, logic and frustration compelled me to find out what was at the top of the stairs that was not responding after my many attempts. So I started walking slowly up the stairs waiting and waiting for someone to answer my calling. I finally reached the top, expecting to see someone. Anyone. It was dark and empty. How can this be?! I checked the room thoroughly and the bathroom as well. Nothing! Was I imagining these distinct footstep sounds?! I even stepped back and forth on the floor to recreate the sound I heard. It definitely came from this room! I went ahead and turned down the room and bathroom upstairs, until I heard noises from downstairs. I peered down the stairs from the top and called out, "Hello? Is someone here?" This time I heard footsteps and then a loud THUMP! I raced down the stairs. No one was there! Now I truly understood why most of the employees were uncomfortable with the 4th floor. With my heart pounding, my mind racing and the hairs on the back of my*

# FLORIDA
*Historic Haunts of the South III*

*neck standing on their end, I quickly finished up the suite so I could get out of there. Before I left I remember blurting out something like, "It's all yours now!" After that incident in the St. Francis suite I found myself trying to trade the 4th floor with other employees so that I did not have to face what was in that room again."*

Megan's story is not unique. Other house keepers have reported similar stories and the reluctance to enter certain rooms. Many of these reports center on activity in the Ponce de Leon and Flagler Suites. Others describe details others have experienced in the hotel, including the sounds of children running up and down the 4th floor (even when none are staying there), lights shutting on and off, locking and unlocking doors and disembodied whispering in the hallways. There are persistent reports of an older man dressed in a fancy 1920s style black and grey suit. There are also reports of a women in white (like the one I experienced). Despite the fact that several paranormal groups have investigated the hotel and captured EVPs and other evidence, the hotel's official policy is that they are not haunted and employees are discouraged from discussing it.

The Casa Monica is easily one of the most detailed and hospitable places to stay in the ancient city. Whether you experience anything at the Casa Monica for yourself or not, it is definitely a must see when in St. Augustine; if only for its beauty and historical qualities. I truly believe (despite the official policy) that it is one of the city's most Historic Haunts!

# PARANORMAL PATRONS AT THE JEFFERSON THEATRE
Site of the Jefferson Theatre, St. Augustine, Florida

Everyone loves going to the theatre. Even in the oldest city with as much as there is to see and do the theatre was a draw. For theatre fans in the greater St. Augustine area, the Jefferson was the place to go.

## The Story of the Jefferson

The Jefferson Theatre was built in 1907 and named for noted thespians Joseph and William Jefferson. It opened as a grand opera house, but also hosted many vaudeville shows. It was the theatre for the well-to-do in town. The distinguished actress Sarah Bernhardt even performed scenes here from "La Dame aux Camelias" and "La Mort de Cleopatra". As time went on the theatre adapted to show silent films and later "talkies".

The beautiful theatre was originally four stories tall and stood at the corner of Cordova and Cathedral Streets. During the silent movie era, the theatre boasted a large roof sign (reportedly lit) with its name. In 1927 a theatre organ was installed. In the 1940s the theatre was even operated by Paramount Pictures Inc.

In 1955 the property was purchased by the St. Augustine National Bank and the theatre was razed to build a new bank. This bank has changed hands several times since. Now visitors to St. Augustine will see a Bank of America branch on the lot where the theatre once stood.

## Tales of the Paranormal

Researching stories for my books I have found that haunted locations have often been the site of unfortunate or noteworthy events. I haven't unearthed any historic evidence of any tragic events that occurred on this site, but it does seem to house some residual energy. Think about this, how many happy memories do you have going to the theatre with your family? I used to work right next to this location and often times felt a certain type of energy around the area and inside the bank.

A few former employees of the bank I interviewed have reported hearing the sound of happy disembodied chatter, and conversations from a spectral group of people. These witnesses never saw anyone and could never tell just what the entities were talking about. One female witness even reported seeing a lady in her 40s in Victorian garb. It seems the theatre is still visited by patrons, even 60 years after it was torn down.

## GEORGIA

# THE WINDSOR'S WINSOME GHOSTS
*Best Western Plus, Windsor Hotel, Americus, Georgia*

Americus is a modest town in Georgia that is a scant 10 miles from the home of former President Jimmy Carter. It is also the international home to Habitats for Humanities, one of the former president's favorite charity organizations.The Windsor Hotel, a glorious piece of late 1800s architecture is located here as well. The hotel, a source of pride for the town, has been recognized with a Georgia Department of Tourism Excellence in Customer Service Award, National Preservation Award and is listed within the National Historic Register of downtown Americus. It is also recognized by paranormal groups in the area and guests at the hotel as a habitat for ghosts.

The Story of the Windsor

The Windsor Hotel was built in 1892 to accommodate northerns heading south during the cold winter months. Its architect modeled it after The Hotel Alcazar in St. Augustine Florida (now Ripley's Believe it or not see Historic Haunts Florida). It featured a hundred room Victorian structure with towers, balconies and a three story open air atrium. At the outset everything seemed great for the lavish hotel, but the 1893 depression affected everything causing many to undergo bankruptcy by the end of the decade. The Windsor (named after one of its operating partners and a local successful businessman) was no exception.

This five story gem was sold in 1893 to jeweler Charles Fricker for $40,000. Fricker renovated the building with electric lights, new elevators, telephones and steam heat. That would help the hotel compete for a while.

The 1930s saw the hotel sell again to Howard Dayton from Daytona Florida who owned many hotels in Florida and Georgia. Dayton kept the Windsor in operation for four decades. On two separate occasions during Dayton's time both Al Capone and John Dillinger reportedly stayed here in the bridal suite with bodyguards posted at the bottom of the stairs. After a glorious run the hotel closed in 1972 after almost 80 years of continous operation. In 1978, the hotel was donated to the city by the Dayton family.

In 1991, after an extensive 6.5 million dollar renovation the hotel reopened, with fifty three individually appointed guest rooms, including six suites, two Tower Suites, the Bridal Suite, and the Carter Presidential Suite (named after our 39th President). In 2010, the hotel underwent another renovation adding modern amenities and features, and restoring many areas of the hotel to its original state. On June 15, 2010, the hotel joined the Best Western Family hosting a re-grand opening with former President Carter and his wife there to cut the ribbon.

There have been reports of paranormal activity at the hotel for quite some time.

# GEORGIA
*The Windsor's Winsome Ghosts*

It is believed that the renovations, as is sometimes the case, may have stirred up whatever still lingers here. Some of the paranormal activity here at the hotel seems to be just residual energy, but there are a few very intelligent haunts here as well.

## The Windsor's Ghostly Guests

In the early 1900s a housekeeper and her daughter lived in the hotel. We don't know all the details, but the woman and her daughter were both pushed down the elevator shaft to their deaths. The young girl is often seen running and playing in the third floor hallway. People often report hearing a little girl laughing and playing followed by footsteps in the hallway. Unusual and sudden temperature change is often experienced in the same hall. Cold spots appear out of nowhere and disappear just as quickly as they came about. Staff and guests have also reported seeing the ghostly reflection of a woman in a large black gown in a mirror on the third floor.

A former doorman, Floyd Lowery, is said to still be here at the hotel as well. He was also the elevator operator and has been seen on the elevator and opening the front door to the hotel. Many have experienced doors opening on their own and they say that Floyd is still on the job. Floyd was an extraordinarily nice man in life and apparently remains so in death. According to the Windsor management Floyd will always be welcome at the hotel.

There are several other reports of paranormal occurrences at the hotel. Kitchen staff at the hotel often report misplaced pots and pans and even a few seen "flying around". They also claim the radio is frequently turned off and on by itself.

There are so many paranormal experiences throughout the entire hotel. The old staircase, the basement, the attic, and numerous other locations throughout the hotel have all had strange activity. The hotel was even thoroughly investigated by a paranormal group in 2006 who claim there was no doubt, this Historic Haunt "IS" haunted. I tend to agree.

*Old Postcard of Windsor Hotel*

**39**

# GEORGIA
*Historic Haunts of the South III*

# THE CURSED PILLAR
*The Cursed Pillar, Augusta Georgia*

Augusta is one of Georgia's most well known cities. Besides being the birthplace of President Woodrow Wilson, James Brown, and sports notables Ty Cobb, Hulk Hogan, and Bobby Jones, its also know for hosting the World's Richest Drag Boat Race and of course the Masters golf tournament. Augusta is also home to one of the most fascinating pieces of urban legend and a Historic Haunt, the so-called "Haunted Pillar"

## The Pillar's Past and the Curse

A farmers market was built in 1830 in Augusta, Georgia. It was here where the locals would come to buy, sell, and trade their goods or just come to socialize and get caught up with their neighbors and towns people. Inconspicuously located amidst the farmers market was a completely unremarkable column which was built to replace one destroyed a year earlier in 1929. This ten foot tall, cracked and chipped column, would soon become quite important and the focus of two different stories claiming it to be cursed.

The first story revolved around a man of God. One day in 1878 a traveling preacher and evangelist came to town and visited the market. He started making several demands of the people. He told them they would build him a church, and told others who would be going to hell for their sins. He made several visits to the market and the people of Augusta quickly grew tired of this man, his demands, and his judgmental preaching. One day they all got together and kicked him out of the market.

In a fit of rage, the preacher stood outside touching one of the buildings pillars and placed a curse on them all. He told them if anyone touched or tried to remove that pillar they would be sorry. After shouting and preaching his final words, he left Augusta. On February 7th, 1878 an unexpected and unseasonal fatal tornado touched down while all were in bed. It wiped out all of the farmers market, except the one pillar the preacher had cursed.

The second explanation for the pillar's curse and much less popular revolves around a time when the area may have housed a slave market. The column reportedly served as a whipping post for misbehaving slaves. Hence the pillar's other nickname the "cursed whipping post". A slave, and alleged voodoo practitioner, after being chained to the column cursed the pillar after receiving his punishment.

In both cases the details of the curse seem to be the same. Anyone attempting to knock it over or destroy it has met with bad luck, grave misfortune or even death! In fact, the pillar's curse seems to have grown to affect those tampering, touching or taunting the pillar as well. Only those attempting to repair, rebuild or move it for positive purposes seem unaffected.

# GEORGIA
*The Cursed Pillar*

## Tempting Fate

Through the years many have tried to remove the pillar through various means. Newspapers and other sources describe the results of these disastrous attempts. Two men attempting to move it were struck by freak lightning and killed on a day with clear skies. A man with a bulldozer planned to use it to knock down the pillar, but was killed when the bulldozer came off the trailer unexpectedly rolling over him and crushing him. Another man, fed up with the whole legend of the pillar, traveled home to retrieve a chain to pull it down with his pickup truck. He was killed on the way in a car accident.

The pillar itself seems to draw bad luck, it was destroyed in 1935 in a bad car accident, but was rebuilt and moved in 1936 to the corner of 5th Street and Broad. In 1958, it was knocked over by a stray cow bale from a passing truck, but was once again re-erected. It has been struck by lightning on at least two other occasions.

Today the pillar still stands at the corner of 5th Street and Broad. Accidents in this area are very high, 39% of the accidents in this part of town happen at this corner near the pillar. Police have executed documented studies trying to figure out why this phenomenon is so high in that area. The speed limit in the area is 25mph/35mph and police have stated how odd it is for the accident rate to be so high in such a low speed zone.

Many still question all of this misfortune truly because of the allegedly cursed pillar? There are skeptics in town who claim the curse is merely the result of a publicity campaign in the early 1900s to drum up tourism for Augusta during the tough times surrounding the Great Depression. However, these same skeptics seem to have no explanation for the unusually high rate of accidents and the continued reports of misfortune occurring to many of the those who touch or tamper with the pillar. The structure still seems to fairly emanate with unusual and paranormal energies. In fact, for the last several decades locals have claimed the pillar itself is haunted. Reports continue to surface of disembodied voices, phantom footsteps, and other unusual materializations.

If you are visiting Augusta, you owe it to yourself to check out this historic pillar. I don't consider myself overly superstitious, but I would think twice before touching it. Then again I don't like to tempt fate. To touch or not to touch this Historic Haunt, I leave that decision to you gentle reader.

# GEORGIA
*Historic Haunts of the South III*

# THE WANDERING GHOST SHIP
*Jekyll Island Ghost Ship, Jekyll Island, GA*

My family and I have taken quite a few short trips together. In most cases we don't go looking for paranormal hot spots or incidents, sometimes they just find us (something which admittedly seems to happen a lot). On this particular trip we spent an afternoon on Jekyll Island off the coast of Georgia. A popular resort area and one I've written about before (Historic Haunts of the South).

As we were driving a huge downpour began. We pulled in to an old house, (well over 100 years old) that is now a book and antique shop. As we went up to the porch the rain started coming down harder and the thunder and lightning got even worse. We started roaming from room to room looking at all the cool stuff and hoping the storm would end. We learned that the building at one time was a sanatorium and was haunted. This provided an interesting footnote which we discussed until the rain stopped (we'll save that for another time).

As we left the antique/book shop we decided to eat at a local restaurant called Blackbeard's which was right on the water. As we were having dinner, another storm rumbled through. Finally the skies started to clear and we decided to walk the beach. My mom and I were looking out at the water and saw what appeared to be an old pirate-style ship way off the coast. We could clearly see three large masts and the fact that it was moving at a slow pace. We turned our heads to get my father's attention and get him to look. When we turned back around to look at the ship, it had totally vanished!! There was no way it could have just sailed out of sight that quickly. We even got in the car and drove around the island, hoping to spot it again, but no ships could be seen anywhere.

After giving up the ship so to speak, we decided to play tourist and head for some of the shops. As we looked through one of the shops we heard the shopkeeper talking about what the storms always bring to the island. I went over to him and asked if he had ever heard anyone report a ghost ship? He asked me what we had seen and I recounted the entire story and as I finished it up he took me over to some matted photos they had for sale and said, "Did it look like this?" I said, "Holy crap thats it!" He started telling us that after every storm many people report seeing a ghost ship off the coast in the area we spotted it. He claimed that apparently in the mid 1800s a three massed ship lost its way during a horrible storm and wrecked. I wondered if this really was its ghost ship?

# GEORGIA
*The Wandering Ghost Ship*

When we returned from our trip I did a little more investigating. The shopkeeper was right, there had been quite a number of people claiming to spot a ghost ship off the coast (perhaps full of paranormal pirates and privateers). Many of these claimed to have captured the ship in photographs. However, many who claimed to have captured the ghost ship have merely captured pictures in the fog of some of the large cargo vessels coming into nearby ports. The difference between the early three masted ships and the cargo vessels is pretty easy to determine in size and outline. This was the first time I had seen a ghost ship of this type, but I'm betting it won't be the last. Sightings of Jekyll Island's ghost ship continue to this day and whenever I'm in the area I try to keep an eye out for this spectral sailing vessel (especially during bad weather). Perhaps next time I'll have my camera handy.

GEORGIA
Historic Haunts of the South III

# SAILOR'S SPIRITS AT THE NAVAL MUSEUM
National Civil War Naval Museum,
Port Columbus, Georgia

The Civil War is a sad, but fascinating chapter in American History. As a history buff, I find myself drawn to locations that tell the stories of this tumultuous time. One of the more interesting is the National Civil War Naval Museum in Port Columbus, Georgia.

## A Little Background on the Museum

The National Civil War Naval Museum houses thousands of archives and artifacts from the Civil War's naval history. Artifacts range from: small momentos of bullets and cannon balls, to actual pieces of ships and ironclads. The museum also houses the largest collection of Civil War and related flags on display in the country. Besides housing these antiques; its the only museum in the U.S. that tells the story of the Civil War navies from the perspective of both sides.

From its humble beginnings at its opening in 1962, the museum has grown, thanks in no small part to generous donations and the draw of additional collection items and displays. In 2001 the museum moved to bigger quarters. Today it comfortably resides on Victory Drive overlooking the Chattahoochee River.

## Notable Displays at the Museum

In May 1863 there was a boiler explosion on the CSS Chattahoochee near Blounstown Florida. Nineteen men died from the accident. The wreckage was recovered and the steam powered sailing vessel underwent repairs. It was put back into service one more time before it was sunk in April 1865. In the 1960s parts of the hull were discovered and brought to the museum. Today they are on display. Other exhibits feature a full scale ship replica of the USS Water Witch, replicas of the USS Hartford including its berth deck, ward room and captain's cabin, and an actual cutter or "ship's boat" from the vessel.

There's also a full scale replica of the USS Monitor's famous turret. The Monitor was a veteran of the world's first combat between ironclads in 1862 against the CSS Virginia (Merrimac). Pieces of the Monitor are also on display. In addition, remains of the CSS Jackson were recovered from the bed of

# GEORGIA
*Sailor's Spirits at the Naval Museum*

the river in the 60s and are on display here at the museum. The museum also showcases the CSS Jackson, the largest surviving Confederate warship. Still, with all these other ships on display, perhaps the most interesting display is the panoramic dockside exhibit that showcases a complete replica exterior and interior of the CSS Albemarle.

## Unusual Paranormal Activity at the Museum

Port Columbus is known to be haunted as it is, but a museum full of artifacts, many of which are related to events associated with war could attract paranormal energies. Besides the stories scared up on the museum's month by month timeline of the war, it has a few haunts of its own. In fact, the museum was even featured on the Bio Channel's My Ghost Story. Ken Johnston, Executive Director of the museum thinks the reason there are paranormal encounters at the museum is because there is "violence, trauma, and death" attached to some of the artifacts.

Among the activity cited by Ken, staff members and visitors for years, are reports of voices and whispers being heard to ear piercing shrieks, and clanking sounds of metal. Further, disembodied voices and sounds have been heard all over the museum. Footsteps have been heard on the wooden deck of the CSS Jackson, phantom bells have been heard ringing on the Albemarle (though no bell is present), and EVPs have been captured.

In addition, people have seen full body apparitions and shadow figures around the relics as well and unknown cold spots with no air ducts around to provide plausible explanation. Apparitions have also been seen in the "captain's room" on the Hartford, and captured on surveillance equipment. In fact, the location has been investigated and similar evidence has been captured with ghost hunting equipment.

Paranormal activity is not concentrated in just the replica ship areas. Display racks near the front of the museum spin uncontrollably sometimes for no apparent reason, books fly of their own free will in the gift shop, and people claim to have been touched with no soul nearby. Some people have also reported strange sensations in the flag gallery and cell phones have frequently turned on and off on their own. One thing is for sure, whether the energy is attached to the actual sailing vessels or to the smaller relics in the museum it doesn't matter, the place is extremely active. Some guests have even captured some of these strange anomalies in their photos when taking souvenir pictures to remember their visit.

To me the National Civil War Naval Museum is a Historic Haunt that I hope to investigate and gather evidence from myself. This not just for the resident spirits, but for the living history on display at every turn. Don't let the ghosts here frighten you away, as the Civil War's Admiral Farragut bravely and famously exclaimed, "Damn the torpedoes, full steam ahead!"

# GEORGIA
*Historic Haunts of the South III*

# MARSHALLED SPIRITS AT THE OLD HOTEL
## Marshall House, Savannah, Georgia

In the 1800s a young woman named Mary Leaver married Colonel James Marshall the 2nd Lieutenant of the Savannah Volunteer Guard. Mary was an energetic entrepreneur and in 1851 she and her father-in-law built the Marshall House, a beautiful grand hotel. In 1857, the proprietor Ralph Meldrim erected the iron veranda that is still seen today. The Marshall House proved to be a social and commercial success.

In 1864 and 1865 the hotel was occupied by Union troops, led by William Tecumseh Sherman, and was used as a Union hospital. The hotel returned to the hospitality business after the end of the Civil War. It was during this time that the hotel hosted Joel Chandler Harris, author of the Uncle Remus Stories. In 1895 the hotel closed down and reopened four years later with electric lights and hot and cold baths.

In 1933 the name of the place was changed to the Gilbert House after a man from Jacksonville, Florida, Herbert Gilbert bought it. It sold again in 1941 and reopened in 1946 after more renovations. It served as an on again off again hotel until 1957 when it closed down for what many thought was the final time. However, in 1999 its nineteenth-century decorations were completely restored. The hotel's name was changed back to the Marshall House, "the oldest hotel in Savannah". During the last 160+ years it has been used as a hospital three times; during the Civil War by the Union and twice during Yellow Fever outbreaks during the 19th century. It has also apparently been used to house a few spirits.

### The Marshall's Multiple Spirits

There are many spirits reported here at the hotel and six members of my Historic Haunts Investigations team have either investigated, visited, or stayed here. The Marshall House has actually been featured on several paranormal television shows due to its high amount of activity. It is believed to be one of the most haunted hotels in Georgia and all of the U.S. Staff members even keep a journal of these high incidents of paranormal activity.

One of the most commonly mentioned topics of paranormal activity reported at the hotel involves children. Children's spirits have been known to play up and down the hallways and have been seen and heard giggling throughout the hotel. This happens even when there are no children staying in or visiting the hotel. They're spirits have been reported by staff, guests, visiting workers

# GEORGIA
*Marshalled Spirits at the Old Hotel*

and paranormal investigation groups. EVPs of the children's laughter have been captured by many.

Besides the children, ghosts of Union Soldiers have been encountered as well. Guests have reported seeing apparitions of Civil War soldiers carrying stretchers and bodies, and others just wandering the halls. Most so realistic and detailed in their physical presentations that guests and staff alike mistook them for re-enactors. There are even numerous reports of one soldier holding his severed arm looking for help to reattach it. It turns out that during the hotel's 1999 renovations workers found human remains under damaged floorboards. After authorities investigated it was discovered the remains belonged to a former patient from the Civil War days. Whether this poor soul is among the hotel's spectral soldiers is unknown.

Other unusual activity has also been reported at the hotel. Many have reported a strange or medicinal odor in the hall when they have walked through. I experienced this personally on more than one occasion and it smelled like a hospital to me.

In addition, faucets and lights have been known to turn on and off on their own accord and when asked to stop, most often times will. Door knobs have been known to rattle with no apparent cause. Loud noises are reported coming from the fourth floor (often when the floor is empty and no obvious explanation is present). Objects in the hotel foyer reportedly move on their

*Marshall House Front*

47

# GEORGIA
*Historic Haunts of the South III*

own. The main floor's ladies restroom contains one particular stall that constantly locks itself, in most cases staff have to come and open it. The apparition of a young woman has been seen in that restroom and might explain some of this activity.

Two other unique experiences have commonly been reported at the hotel. The first involves the former room of Joel Chandler Harris (it was from his stories that the hard to find, but famous Song of the South was created). The disembodied sounds of typing and a moving typewriter have been reported coming from this room.

The second frequently reported incident - perhaps another paranormal experience tied to the Marshall House's days as a hospital - involves examinations. Many guests have reported waking in the middle of the night with their arms outstretched as if medical personnel were pulling them out to check their pulse. Hopefully, whoever or whatever was doing this was happy to find their "patients" were still alive.

On your next visit to Savannah, have lunch or dinner at the Pirate's House (featured in Historic Haunts of the South II) and stay at the Marshall House. You'll experience two of Savannah's most notoriously haunted locations and you'll discover great food and a hotel that has won Preservation and Best of Savannah Awards. You may even experience something paranormal yourself. Regardless, it will be a hauntingly good trip.

# GEORGIA

*The Haunts of Orange Hall*

# THE HAUNTS OF ORANGE HALL
*Orange Hall, St. Marys, Georgia*

*Orange Hall*

Thirty eight miles north of Jacksonville, Florida lies the town of St. Marys, Georgia. The area is noteworthy for its coastal and naval affiliations. Nearby Kings Bay Naval Base houses Nuclear Submarines, and the town has a submarine museum. St. Marys is the gateway to Cumberland Island, known for its population of wild horses, scenic nature, and status as the longest of Georgia's Barrier Islands. St. Marys is also the home to one of Georgia's most beautiful and Historic Haunts, Orange Hall.

## The Origins of Orange Hall

Horace Southworth Pratt came to St. Marys Georgia in 1820. He was a graduate from Yale University, and the Princeton Theological Seminary, a young missionary who was eager to begin his life's work. Reverend Pratt helped organize the First Presbyterian Church across the street from where he would later build his home. In 1829, his first wife Jane and his father-in-law John Wood both died unexpectedly.

After his first wife's death, Pratt stayed in St. Marys and later remarried. He also named at least one of his children with his second wife Jane in honor of his first wife. He would later lose this daughter at the early age of eight (there

# GEORGIA
*Historic Haunts of the South III*

may have been as many as three "Jane Pratts" to have passed). Pratt decided to build a home with the money inherited from his first wife and father-in-law. The beautiful white home he had Isaac Slayton construct still sits just across the street from the church.

The house is thought to be the first (and possibly best) example of Greek Revival Design in America. Unfortunately, Pratt would never really get a chance to settle in and enjoy his home. He had made an earlier promise to teach at the University of Alabama if no other suitable candidates could be found. The University called him out on his promise and being a man of his word, he kept his promise moving to Alabama as his home was in the final stages of completion.

Pratt kept his property in St. Marys. Military General Duncan Lamont Clinch rented Orange Hall from Pratt when he departed for Alabama and may have been the first to occupy the house. Pratt unexpectedly passed away in 1840. The property was later sold at auction in 1846. Many people have owned the property since Pratt's death. Over time the building would house many noteworthy owners and their families including a wealthy planter and a mayor of St. Marys.

During the Civil War, Orange Hall was occupied by the Union Army and for some unknown reason, they never destroyed the building. In the 1930s S.C. Townsend purchased the property and turned the upper floors into apartments. In 1951, Kraft Corporation purchased the property and used it and its separate apartments to house their mill employees.

The city purchased Orange Hall in 1965 and it is now a museum and wedding venue. It was listed on the National Register of Historic Places in May 1973. Orange Hall is considered one of Georgia's ten most "endangered historic sites". Many have inquired why the property wasn't called Pratt Mansion or Pratt Hall and the reason is because of all the orange trees on the property. Many have called it something else as well...haunted!

## Orange Hall's Haunts

It is said that there may be as many as six spirits roaming this beautiful old home. I have been here many times since my first trip in 2002. I can tell you with certainty that I have come into contact with at least two of them.

One spirit residing here is said to be young Jane Pratt. When she died at an early age she actually wasn't even in this county, but is seems she returned to her childhood home. Many say she is the one that moves the toys and the dolls, especially the doll with three faces. (Believe me, that thing is creepy!) Many ghostly faces and figures have been reported and photographed in little Jane's room. Her spirit has been seen walking through the building, and is sometimes active during the midnight hour. The appearance of her ghost has

*The Haunts of Orange Hall*

sometimes been marked by light flashes and unusual images.

She appears to be between the ages of 6 and 8 and I believe I came in contact with her on my very first trip here. While walking through the building, I kept feeling someone tugging at my pant leg. It was as if a child were trying to get my attention. I inquired with one of the museum workers and they said this ghostly behavior is reported often, especially in the upstairs room where the toys are (and that is where it happened).

There are also reports of an elderly man and woman here. I have smelled rose water (or an old style perfume) and have heard the disembodied sounds of a woman humming. As for the male presence reported, I have never come in contact with him.

Besides Jane's ghost, others have witnessed activity in the kitchen area and around the fireplace. The area or item most commonly reported having a presence near it is the three faced baby doll. The faces on the doll are different expressions and to me, all are creepy (but admittedly I hate porcelain dolls).

Additional reports about manifestations at Orange Hall describe apparitions of past owners spotted on the right side of the house and the spirits of servants spotted in the basement and other areas. Orange Hall is very paranormally active and has been investigated by many paranormal groups because of it. These groups and individuals have reported numerous incidents of strange sounds, disembodied noises, high K-2 meter activity, plentiful EVPs, and inexplicable extreme temperature changes. Some of this activity is apparently prevalent on the properties grounds as well.

Most paranormal groups who have investigated have come to the same conclusion as the good people of St. Marys. Orange Hall is haunted! It is a must see if you are in or traveling through southeast Georgia. However, if you're a paranormal fan it isn't the only haunted hot spot in St. Marys. You may want to poke around a bit more.

## GEORGIA
*Historic Haunts of the South III*

# ST. SIMON'S GHOSTLY KEEPER
*St. Simon's Island Lighthouse,*
*St. Simons Island, Georgia*

*St. Simon's Lighthouse*

I have a great respect and admiration for lighthouses and lightkeepers. It was through their devoted and united efforts that many boats and sailors were able to avoid dangerous waters and return safely. At one lighthouse in St. Simons, however, discord between lighthouse keepers not only lead to murder, it led to a well known Historic Haunt.

### Story of a Lighthouse

The story of the St. Simon's Lighthouse begins with John Couper, a plantation owner on St. Simon's. On October 17, 1804 Couper deeded four acres of land known as "Couper's Point" at the south end of the island for one dollar to the federal government for the construction of a lighthouse. In 1807, the Treasury Department hired James Gould of Massachusetts to build the lighthouse and a residence for the keepers. The first St. Simon's Lighthouse was built in 1810 of mostly "tabby" (a mixture of oyster, shell, lime, sand and water) with some brick. It was eighty-five feet tall. President Madison appointed Gould its first keeper in May of 1810, a post he would hold until 1837 when he retired.

The lighthouse performed its duties faithfully until the coming of the Civil War. With the advancing of Federal Troops in the area, the retreating Confederates decided in 1862 to destroy the lighthouse rather than see it fall into the hands of the Union. The once bright lighthouse stood no more.

# GEORGIA
*St. Simon's Ghostly Keeper*

With the Civil War over, the U.S. Government decided to move ahead with plans for a second lighthouse located west of the first. This lighthouse featured a 104 foot tall tower, 129 step cast-iron spiral staircase, and a new keeper's house. It was completed in the early 1870s and overhauled and improved in 1876.

## The Keepers' Quarrel

In March of 1880 an incident occurred that would forever mark this lighthouse in both the living and "unliving" sense. On that date there was a quarrel between main keeper Frederick Osborne and his assistant keeper John Stephens. The quarrel came about according to most stories for one of two reasons (although it may have been a little of both). In one version of the story Stephens reportedly made unwanted advances on Osborne's wife. In the other Osborne made exceedingly inappropriate remarks about Stephen's wife. Whatever the real reasons, the outcome was the same at 98 feet at the top of the tower, there was a duel and Osborne was killed. Stephens was arrested and charged with murder, but a jury later acquitted him.

## St. Simon's Lifesaving Continues

The lighthouse continued its operations after the deadly duel. As progress and technology improved so did the lighthouse. In 1934 the kerosene light was replaced with electricity. In 1953 the lighthouse was automated and the last lightkeeper retired. The tower underwent restorations in 1989 and 1997. Today the lighthouse is still in operation and is operated jointly by the U.S. Coast Guard and Coastal Georgia Historical Society.

## Paranormal Tales of the Lighthouse

Paranormal activity in the lighthouse began immediately after the infamous duel. Stephens reported hearing heavy phantom footsteps in the tower after Osborne's death. Osborne's ghost has been seen, felt and heard in and around the tower. In fact, the wives of several lightkeepers reported hearing footsteps and encountering Osborne's spirit. His spirit reportedly constantly harassed keeper Svendsen's family dog, and on at least one occasion aided a keeper's wife when her husband was gone. This keeper's wife was reportedly unable to get the lighthouse equipment to work in bad weather and hearing phantom footsteps in the tower implored Osborne's ghost to assist her. Immediately after that the seized up equipment miraculously and mysteriously freed up.

Tales of the presence of keeper Osborne's spirit continue. Coast Guardsmen doing maintenance have repeatedly reported phantom footsteps. This regularly reported activity has enticed paranormal teams to investigate and they and other individuals have reported capturing EVPs and recording footsteps on their audio recorders.

# GEORGIA
*Historic Haunts of the South III*

## Other Spirits at the Lighthouse

Keeper Osborne's death is not the only misfortune the lighthouse has seen. There was also a suicide reported in August of 1999 when a woman jumped from the tower. People have reported seeing a female ghost walking at the top of the tower and a strong feeling of sadness.

The keeper's house is very old and has had some paranormal activity reported as well. A major restoration effort took place here in 2010 and the lighthouse and the keeper's quarters are gorgeous. However, this may have further stirred up the spirits.

## My Paranormal Experiences at the Lighthouse

When I visited here several years ago, I felt a presence in the house, but more so in the tower. I kept hearing footsteps behind me in the tower. I literally thought someone was behind me and kept stopping to move out of the way as I climbed to the top, but when I turned and looked back I realized there was no one in the tower with me. After descending I asked the staff member at the base of the tower and she said no one else had been in there for over an hour.

The St. Simon's Lighthouse is a wonderful structure and I can't wait to return again and experience it. This gorgeous lighthouse also boasts a beautiful view. Its frequent reports of paranormal activity have made it a staple of local ghost tours, and it is considered one of the Top 15 Haunted Lighthouses in America. Make sure to check this Historic Haunt out the next time you are in the area.

## KENTUCKY

# BROWN'S SPECTRE INN ATTENDANCE
*Inn at Woodhaven, Louisville, Kentucky*

One third of all bourbon whiskey comes from Louisville! Louisville is known for whiskey and many things, the Derby, the largest Beatles festival in the world, Kentucky Fried Chicken, and the best bats in the U.S., the Louisville slugger. Louisville is also home to some amazing sites, both picturesque and paranormal. One of these fascinating and scenic places is the Inn at Woodhaven.

Woodhaven was originally known as Woodview when it was built in 1853 by Theodore Brown. The area was known as low Dutch Station due to a fort that was on the original property near Beargrass Creek, and Brown had inherited it from his father. Brown created his mansion on his 500 acre tract and incorporated a gothic revival style that may have been borrowed from two well known architects, A.J. Downing and Jacob Beaverson.

Regardless, the structure and its conception had many unique qualities including diamond window panes, interior shutters, and 14 foot arched gothic doors. Brown, a prominent and well know progressive farmer, planted several indigenous trees on the 18 acres in front of the house (several of Brown's letters on landscape architecture are in the Smithsonian today). Brown lived here, marrying twice, and raising a total of twenty children on the property.

In 1920, the Monohan family bought the property and changed the name to Woodhaven. They also owned the property known as Wildwood which had been owned by Theodore's brother James. The Monohans sold both properties in the 1970s and Woodhaven was almost razed in 1985, but was saved by St. Matthews.

In 1986 Bob Drane bought the property and spent three years restoring it. Marsha Burton purchased the property in 1993 and added Rose Cottage another structure that borrowed heavily from the architectural details and influences of the main building. Today the Inn at Woodhaven is listed on the National Register of Historic Places and is considered one of Kentucky's premier Inns and a county landmark. Guests of the Inn are treated not only to delicious breakfasts, comfortable rooms and gracious hospitality; occasionally they're treated to some paranormal activity.

Woodhaven's Resident Haunts.

Many believe the extensive restoration efforts throughout the years may have contributed to the paranormal encounters reported in the house. The main spirit believed to reside here is none other than Theodore Brown himself. A male apparition has been seen here by multiple guests on many different occasions. Many guests were surprised to discover the ghost they encountered matched the portrait of Brown. One guest, after describing her

# KENTUCKY
*Historic Haunts of the South III*

encounter of a male apparition on the front porch, saw the portrait of Brown and like the others stated, "That's him!" Brown's spirit isn't malicious; he just seems to still be keeping a watchful eye on his beloved home.

There are other incidents of paranormal activity at the Inn at Woodhaven, but its impossible to know if these are the result of Brown's ghost. Two of the "staff" members, "Phoebe" the dog and "Baby" the cat may have more of a clue as animals are more sensitive to this type of activity. If they know they certainly aren't telling. Fans of the paranormal will find this an amazing and centrally located place to stay while taking in some of the other nearby haunts (Waverly Hills Sanitorium [Historic Haunts of the South], Jack Daniel's Distillery, or even Old Talbott's Tavern [both in Historic Haunts of the South II]. If you go to Marsha Burton and her excellent staff will be happy to host you and Theodore Brown might even look in on you.

LOUISIANA

# THE GRACIOUS GHOST OF MRS. BAUGHMAN
*Edgewood Plantation, Farmerville, Louisiana*

Located one mile west of Farmerville, Louisiana on Highway 2 is a fabulously restored structure that was once known as one of Louisiana's Grand Mansions, the Edgewood Plantation. Edgewood Plantation, also known as the Baughman House, was built in 1902 by Jefferson Davis Baughman on eight beautiful acres with towering trees. This Queen-Anne Style, Victorian beauty was complete with a bell tower/turrant room and thirteen rooms with high ceilings, hardwood floors, and beautiful crown moulding. Today, thanks to extensive restoration efforts she's a beauty and draws attention because of her rich history, appearance and resident haunts.

## The Brief Story of Edgewood Plantation

J.D. Baughman lived here with his wife Nancy and their four daughters. Their oldest daughter, Faye, was the last one to live here until her death in the late 1970s. After Ms. Faye's death, the house sat vacant for many years and began to decay. Even worse the woods began to take over the grounds and almost obscured the view of all but the top parts of the building, that is until Pat and Kay Carroll bought the home in 2010 and began a beautiful restoration process. After the renovations they began to call themselves the newest oldest place in town.

The Edgewood Plantation Bed and Breakfast opened in 2012. It wasn't long before the beauty of the place, the amazing food and hospitality caused a stir throughout the Parrish. Something else also drew attention, apparently the renovations stirred up someone or something from the past, providing the inn with at least one paranormal guest.

## The Spirits of the Edgewood

One of the spirits thought to be still lingering here is believed to be Mrs. Baughman herself. Apparently her spirit likes to interact with guests and investigators and has made her presence known to many. People have heard voices at the bed and breakfast, heard footsteps, seen shadow figures, and have received responses when using paranormal detection devices and flashlights. In fact, the Bed and Breakfast and the grounds have been investigated several times. It has been suggested that the plantation is haunted because the family cemetery is located right across the street.

There is a place in the cemetery where JD Baughman is buried where people can sit and pay their respects. His wife reportedly visited him every single day until her death because she grieved the loss of her husband so badly. Some say she even packed her lunch and would sit by his grave, have her lunch, and talk with him for hours. People have reported seeing strange things in the cemetery.

It seems that some of the discussion surrounding activity near the house and in the cemetery might be due to a local legend. According to this legend a young lady was embalmed under glass, which was then covered in concrete. The legend mentions that cracks in the concrete have caused openings that allow people to view the woman within. Her spirit allegedly still haunts the cemetery as well. However, after extensive research I have been unable to corroborate it as anything less than local lore. In the meantime, reports of paranormal activity involving the Edgewood Plantation and the possible spirit of Mrs. Baughman continue.

If Mrs. Baughman's spirit truly is residing in the refurbished bed and breakfast, then Pat and Kay Carroll have more than they bargained for. Not only do they have a beautiful establishment and wedding locale on their hands, they also have a splendid home registered with the National Register of Historic Places and a gorgeous Historic Haunt. They say love never dies and if Mrs. Baughman is back perhaps its because she, like the guests that stay here, love the place and feel compelled to keep coming back.

# THE GANGSTERS GHOSTS: BONNIE & CLYDE STILL TOGETHER?

**Bonnie and Clyde Death Site,
Hwy 154 Gibsland, Louisiana**

During the harsh times of the Great Depression, and the violence of the "Public Enemy Era" (1931-1935), no two outlaws captured the public's attention like Bonnie and Clyde. The exploits that made them famous would eventually lead to their deaths. However, it would also help them achieve legendary pop culture status via a 1967 movie about their lives starring Warren Beatty and Faye Dunaway.

*Bonnie & Clyde*

### Boy Meets Girl

Bonnie Elizabeth Parker dropped out of school shortly before her sixteenth birthday and married a man named Ray Thornton on September 25, 1926. The marriage wouldn't last as Thornton frequently disappeared and eventually after 1929 crossed paths with his wife again (they were never divorced and she was wearing the ring when she was killed). After her marriage deteriorated Parker moved in with her mother taking a job as a waitress in a Dallas cafe. One of her regular customers was then postal worker Ted Hinton (who would later join the Dallas Sheriff's department and be part of the posse that later killed her). She was restless in her job and her life of desperate poverty. It caused her to develop a strong contempt for authority. All of these qualities she found in common with a young man she met (according to most credible accounts) on January of 1930 at the age of 19. They were both immediately smitten.

The object of her affection was 21 year old habitual criminal Clyde Chestnut Barrow. By the time they met he already had a history of cracking safes, robbing stores and stealing cars. After arrests in 1928 and 1929 and shortly after meeting Bonnie, Clyde was sent to Eastham Prison Farm in April 1930. He was paroled in February 1932. Prison had changed him into a hardened criminal. He swore never to go back to prison and Bonnie vowed to die with him if need be.

### The Barrow's Gang Crime Spree

Bonnie and Clyde would be the fixture of a rotating group of accomplices that would include Ralph Fults, Raymond Hamilton, W.D. Jones, Marvin "Buck" Barrow (Clyde's brother) and his wife Blanche among others. The gang would move from petty thievery to bank robberies, kidnapping and murder, reportedly killing as many as

# LOUISIANA
*Historic Haunts of the South III*

13 (9 of which were believed to be cops). The gang was cornered many times, but Clyde managed to shoot his way out with his favorite weapon the Browning Automatic Rifle.

While they frequently escaped it was not without injury, some gang members were shot or captured, and Clyde and Bonnie both received injuries. During the crime spree they kidnapped several robbery victims only to release them later. Coincidentally, one of these was H.D. Darby, a young undertaker who Bonnie remarked might someday be working on her! He would later help identify her body and help in her embalming.

## Bonnie and Clyde's Last Runs

The Barrow's Gang would often have to make runs for supplies and hide out with family members in between crime sprees. Clyde made sure to keep the gang moving and would skirt the edges of five midwestern states taking advantage of the "state line" rule preventing officers from pursuing criminals into another department's jurisdiction (this of course before the FBI later consolidated efforts in similar cases).

In January of 1934, Clyde orchestrated the "Eastham Breakout" freeing Raymond Hamilton, Henry Methvin and several others (an act of revenge on Clyde's part for the treatment he received while imprisoned in the Texas Penal system). After the shooting of a prison officer during the escape, the Texas Department of Corrections contacted Captain Frank A. Hamer, a former Texas Ranger, and persuaded him to hunt down the Barrows Gang. Hamer would become the gang's shadow typically a town or two behind them at most.

On April 1, 1934 (Easter Sunday) Clyde and Henry Methvin killed two young highway patrolmen. The Dallas daily papers seized on the story, exaggerating the details and eyewitness accounts and causing a public outcry demanding the deaths of the Barrows gang members once and for all. A reward was offered for their dead bodies.

## The Ambush

Hamer had been narrowing in on the gang with his posse members from Texas [B.M. "Manny" Gault, Bob Alcorn, and Ted Hinton (Bonnie's once customer)]. He learned that Bonnie and Clyde were planning on going to Bienville Parish in Gibsland, Louisiana. He recruited two Louisiana officers, Henderson Jordan and Prentiss Morel Oakley and they waited in ambush on a road deep in the piney Louisiana woods.

*The bullet riddled V8*

At Approximately 9:15 a.m. on May 23, the posse heard a Ford V8 stolen by Clyde approaching at high speed. The lawmen opened fire unleashing a combined total of 130 rounds in a barrage of gunfire so loud they suffered temporary deafness all afternoon. Oakley fired first killing Clyde instantly with a fatal head shot. Some reports claim that Bonnie and Clyde were shot more than fifty times. The official report listed 26 separate entrance wounds on Bonnie's body and 17 on Clydes. Because of the number of bullet holes, the undertaker would later have trouble embalming the bodies.

# LOUISIANA

*The Gangsters Ghosts: Bonnie & Clyde Still Together?*

Upon approaching the car the officers found Bonnie's body slumped over Clyde's. They also discovered an arsenal of rifles, sawed off shotguns, assorted handguns, some 15 sets of license plates from a variety of states and thousands of rounds of ammunition.

## The Aftermath

The posse began sifting through items in the car. Hamer kept the guns and ammo and a box of fishing tackle (part of his compensation package with the Texas DOC). Other posse members took Bonnie's clothing and personal effects and items belonging to Clyde. Sheriff Jordan was rumored to have purchased land in Acadia and an auction barn from a suitcase full of cash he kept. He also tried to keep the death car, but it was returned to its original owner. The posse's biggest reward would be the sale of the collected memorabilia they grabbed as state, county and other organizations reneged on most of the reward money.

*Ammunition and other items found in the car*

Gault and Acorn were left to guard the bodies, while the others reported the deaths to their supervisors. However, they didn't expect the circus-like atmosphere as a crowd soon gathered and attempted to claim souvenirs. People were collecting shell casings, slivers of glass from the car window, cutting off bloody pieces of Bonnie's hair and dress, and some reportedly even tried to cut off Clyde's ear and trigger finger. The returning officers and coroner put an end to the madness and moved people back. The car was towed from the site with the bodies still in the vehicle.

Despite their desire to be buried together, Bonnie's family held a funeral and interned her at a different location than Clyde. Her funeral drew more than 20,000 people. She allegedly received flowers and cards from Pretty Boy Floyd, John Dillinger, and a group of Dallas city newsboys (her sudden demise had sold over 500,000 newspapers in Dallas alone). The life insurance policies of Bonnie and Clyde were paid in full after their deaths (a policy change since then of course excludes pay outs for deaths caused by criminal acts).

The bullet-riddled Ford that the lovers were driving when ambushed gained notoriety and became a popular traveling attraction at flea markets, fairs and amusement parks. It was sold to a Las Vegas car museum in the 1980s. Today the car can be found on display at Whiskey Pete's in Primm, Nevada.

The location of the ambush is commemorated by a stone marker, which unfortunately has been ravaged by souvenir hunters so badly that is almost illegible. A small metal version was added to accompany the stone marker, but has been stolen (as has its replacement) sever-

*Ambush Site Marker Courtesy of Wikimedia Commons*

61

# LOUISIANA
*Historic Haunts of the South III*

al times. Like the mad souvenir hunters of Gibsland its hard not to be drawn to the story of these two outlaws. However, fans of the paranormal may be drawn to the ambush site for other reasons.

## Apparitions and More at the Ambush Site

At the site of Parker and Barrow's ambush, many have reported strange occurrences pretty much since their deaths. Many who have stopped here have reported hearing the sounds of dozens, maybe even hundreds of bullets being fired. Others have felt a sense of sorrow or death. Some have even reported the feeling of being watched from the tree line like the police did on that fateful day.

Paranormal groups and those curious have reported a variety of activity. EVP's have been captured, and strange mists and anomalies have appeared in photos of the general area. Photographs of the markers themselves have sometimes been known to appear with inexplicable ghostly forms and apparitions. Interestingly enough, despite the time of the ambush, the site is rumored to be more active at night (especially during a full moon).

Even if you don't experience anything paranormal here, this is a very important piece of American gangster history. The town of Gibsland commemorates the anniversary of the ambush every year with a "Bonnie and Clyde Festival". Like the people of the town, the story of this notorious couple, and the site of the ambush, is a Historic Haunt that's hard not to revisit.

# THE PROPHETIC VOODOO PRIESTESS AND THE SWAMP

*Manchac Swamp and Voodoo Priestess Julie Brown, Laplace, Louisiana*

*Manchac Swamp*

Located near the west shore of Lake Ponchatrain, over the tracks of the Illinois Central Railroad, and by a junction of Highway 55 North, lies an interesting piece of real estate. Interesting not only because it houses the third largest bridge in the world, but because of something else. Staring deep into the area the glare of red eyes might alert you to the crocodiles around you, along with the sounds of the Bayou and the other creatures here as well. All of whom call this place, Manchac Swamp, home.

Manchac Swamp is a very unnerving and eerie area that's been nicknamed the "haunted swamp". There is apparently really only one way in and one way out (safely anyway). Cajun Pride Tours offers tours of the area and tells travelers the history and tales of the area, but you might want to hear a few of these tales before you head into the swamps.

## Tales of the Swamp

The first story you might find unsettling is that of the Rougarou. What the heck is that you might ask? Legend has it that the Rougarou is a Cajun werewolf creature, similar to a Bigfoot, but much nastier. The Rougarou reportedly bears a strong resemblance to a Sasquatch with glowing eyes and a taste for the meat of the swamp denizens. It has even been reported to attack people, but admittedly this usually just to scare them away. Reports of this creature have persisted for years and continue to this

# LOUISIANA
*Historic Haunts of the South III*

day.

If you don't believe in the Rougarou, then there is something else to worry about and perhaps take more seriously. The ghost of voodoo priestess Julie Brown (sometimes mentioned as Julie White). Her spirit has been sighted here numerous times over the last several decades. During her living days many people in town feared Ms. Julie Brown because she practiced something they didn't understand. However, on many occasions she helped the sick recover with her herbal concoctions. To many of these people and related townsfolk she was friendly "Aunt Julie". As a rare land-owning woman of color, the residents of the area (mostly German immigrants) respected her. As a healer and member of the community they adored her, but as a singer they feared her!

## Aunt Julie and Her Disturbing Lyrics

Aunt Julie lived in and owned land in Frenier Beach (not really a beach) and this town along with its neighboring towns Ruddock and Wagram, all only four miles apart, had become somewhat prosperous in the early 1900s. Ruddock benefitted from the thriving lumber industry and was distinct with its buildings, horse stables, offices and city-length sidewalks of wood all resting comfortably above the swamp on wooden stilts.

Wagram and Frenier Beach specialized in barrel stave manufacturing and cabbage farming. Both were easily able to ship the cabbage out in their own barrels via the nearby railroad. So here too prosperity was found.

Travelers, workers, and locals in these towns and around the railways would often share tales of Julie Brown and her supernatural gifts. Among them, a very disturbing talent for predicting the destruction of neighboring towns, especially in song. In fact, she would sing disturbing songs from the front porch of her house for all to hear. To the townspeople perhaps the most disturbing was the one she sang the most... "One day I'm gonna die, and I'm gonna take all of you with me." She would sing this with a smile and a diabolical gleam in her eye. Sometimes she added the town names in at the end. While Wagram and Ruddock were mentioned, the town where she had her home, Frenier Beach was added in the most.

One day in the fall of 1915 as she lay dying, she was said to have cursed the town of Frenier with her song. She again started singing songs of taking the town with her when she died. Julie Brown passed and the town insisted on paying their respects. As her body was being put in the ground in her coffin, the Great West Indies Storm (estimated to have been a category three hurricane) blew through the area. The high speed winds snatched up her coffin and hurled it deep into the Louisiana Bayou. It also blew the funeral attendees and all other townspeople around along with animals and anything else around. The storm killed hundreds of people and flooded, battered and decimated the three villages.

After the storm Aunt Julia's body was recovered deep in the swamp (although the coffin was never found). She was given a proper burial and the townspeople who perished during the storm were buried in a mass grave in Manchac Swamp near hers. Since then Frenier Beach has tried to come back as a Lakefront resort, but business was always ruined by the periodic unexpected storm, the erosion and damage from it, and the occasional body that washed up. Frenier's failures have been blamed on the

# LOUISIANA
*The Prophetic Voodoo Priestess and the Swamp*

curse, the ghost of the voodoo priestess, and the abundant reports of supernatural activity in the swamp.

## The Haunted Swamp

Many claim to have seen the spirit of Julie in Manchac Swamp or have heard her singing her song "One day I'm gonna die, and I'm gonna take all of you with me." Others have reported hearing the victims who died during the storm screaming. Frequent apparitions and shadow forms have been reported, as well as other paranormal phenomenon. The activity has occurred enough to draw several paranormal teams to investigate, and they too often seem to capture unusual evidence. No one knows whether all of this activity can be attributed to Julie Brown's voodoo practices and curses or to other sources. Either way, the swamps can be a bit eerie at times, but for me are a must see on any trip to Louisiana, and especially to New Orleans.

**SIDEBAR:**

Now, since we're discussing Voodoo, I've done a little research on this topic from time to time. (no small wonder since I am related to voodoo priestess Marie Laveau.) Florida Water has been used for a very long time in voodoo rituals as a cleansing agent. There is a quote about Florida Water that states "Voodoo smells great!" Murray and Lanman's created Florida Water cologne in 1808. It is used in Santeria to bless or for honoring someone. It has been referred to as a liquid quartz crystal for cleansing. I actually started using this after an investigation as a precautionary measure to make sure nothing followed me home. You might want to pick up a bottle just in case you visited the haunted Manach swamp.

65

## LOUISIANA
*Historic Haunts of the South III*

# THE MOST HAUNTED CEMETERY IN THE WORLD

## St. Louis Cemetery #1, New Orleans, Louisiana

Located in the "Treme" neighborhood, one block from the French Quarter and eight blocks from the Mississippi River is one of the most famous spots in all of New Orleans. Visitors tour this place every day and often bring tokens of their esteem. And why not, according to legend those tokens and the right markings and message might grant you wishes from the "Voodoo Queen" herself, Marie Laveau at her tomb in St. Louis Cemetery #1.

St. Louis Cemetery #1 is the most famous of the three St. Louis Cemeteries. It opened in 1789 (after a huge fire in 1788 caused a redesign). The cemetery is well known for its above ground vaults constructed mostly in the 18th and 19th centuries, Those vaults, contrary to popular belief, owe more of their design and appearance to French and Spanish tradition than they do to issues with the water levels in New Orleans. While these vaults certainly draw the attention of visitors to the cemetery, so too do the noteworthy people buried there now and in the future.

Despite the cemetery only covering one square block, there are over a thousand buried here. The most famous person who is buried here is the great Voodoo Priestess Marie Laveau and Delphine LaLaurie (a cruel and twisted woman and slave owner). Nicholas Cage is said to have even purchased a pyramid shaped tomb for his future grave site.

Cemetery #1 has proven to be popular not only to actors choosing their final resting place, but Hollywood in general. The Cincinnati Kid (1965) and the legendary Easy Rider (1969) were both filmed here. After Easy Rider though filming was mostly limited to pre-approved documentaries (one notable exception being 1994's Interview with the Vampire). Because of the cemetery's popularity new rules have been recently set in place regarding the cemetery. Visitors must be accompanied by a licensed tour guide. Families of the deceased, tomb owners and genealogists can apply for special passes.

Whether you take the tour to see this landmark cemetery or not you will soon learn that New Orleans has other old and famed burial sites. St. Louis Cemetery #2 opened in 1823 and is located just three blocks away and St. Louis #3 was opened in 1854, but is three miles away. Regardless of the one you visit, they are all reported to be haunted.

### The Voodoo Queen and Paranormal Activity

There is one very famous spirit said to walk among the tombs and that is Marie Laveau. Many have reported seeing her spirit in the cemetery dancing and performing rituals. In addition to Laveau's grave site, it is said that a mysterious crow watches over her grave and is supposedly seen on a daily basis. I've never seen the crow, but

# LOUISIANA
*The Most Haunted Cemetery in the World*

this cemetery definitely holds a feeling all its own. Perhaps because I felt a connection with Laveau since she is an ancestor of mine (distant cousin).

Besides Marie Laveau's ghost, there has been a multitude of other activity reported. The apparition of phantom figures, shadows, Civil War soldiers, and yellow fever victims have all been seen numerous times, along with the ghosts of animals (typically dogs and cats). Further, visitors here frequently reported the sounds of eerie screams inside the tombs, orbs and unusual lights, mists, and disembodied voices and whispering.

Not all of these reports chronicle stories of scary paranormal activity. In true New Orleans fashion, some reflect the jubilant nature of their funeral processions. These reports claim that some of the activity coming from this cemetery are of a lively nature. Several witnesses have stated at times late at night it sounds like a wild jazz party coming from inside the cemetery. The sounds of trumpets and saxophones can be heard and people have even called the police about the noise, but when they arrive, the party seems to be over. Apparently St. Louis Cemetery #1 is a swinging place for the dead. I have to admit, if I was going to haunt a cemetery this would be the one to haunt. I recommend you take a tour and experience this Historic Haunt and slice of New Orleans culture for yourself.

**Note:**

While I don't practice Santeria, I'd be remiss if I didn't mention a few last things about St. Louis Cemetery #1. Legend claims that at Marie Laveau's tomb you can awaken her by knocking three times. If you leave an offering to her, mark three "X's" on her tomb, and knock three times again. She may grant you a wish or give you some of her power. The city of course frowns on this practice, but its obvious from the tomb that many still do it. In addition, if you find a small statuary of a monkey and a rooster together, take it, its meant for you and it brings good luck.

*Charles Talen Own image*
*Licensed through wikimedia/creative commons 4.0*

**67**

NORTH CAROLINA

# SPIRITS ABOUND AT BARLEY'S TAPROOM

*Barley's Taproom, Asheville, North Carolina*

Asheville, North Carolina is a bustling mecca for the craft beer and tourism industries. Barley's Taproom, located in the arts and entertainment district is a mainstay of the Asheville Pub Scene and one of the area's most popular establishments. It is recognized as the Best Taproom in the South (Southern Draught Beer News) and a Top Ten in the South (Celebrator Beer Magazine). To those interested in the paranormal its not only a great place to grab a craft pint, its also a very haunted pub.

*Barley's Taproom*

### The Barley's Area Background

Barley's Taproom was originally an appliance store in the 1920s and reportedly not far from the early town gallows. It didn't become Barley's until 1994. Before Barley's, this 8,000 square foot space was the location of the well known craft brewing company Highland Brewing. Before Highland, the area was well known for other more unsavory reasons.

On the thirteenth of November, 1906, inmate Will Harris (a fugitive from Charlotte) broke free from a chain gain and headed for Asheville. The details of this story get a little uncertain at this point as some claim Harris was looking for his ex-grilfriend Molly Maxwell, others claim she was nothing more than an acquaintance and that he was acting erratic anyway. Regardless, Harris' behavior drew the attention of locals (including Maxwell's sister) who eventually called the police. While the police were responding, Harris got his hands on a rifle and alcohol and went on a killing spree, forever marking this area as Asheville's largest mass murder site. Harris started shooting anything in sight and telling people he was the Devil. He killed five people in all including two responding police officers, and wounded many others including a neighborhood dog which ultimately passed as well.

# NORTH CAROLINA
*Spirits Abound at Barley's Taproom*

In some reports of the events of that day Harris took his own life, in others the story ended quite differently. The local citizens went searching for Harris with a posse of over 1,000 men. They found him in a thicket in nearby Fletcher. They fired over 100 bullets gunning him down in the process. In 1907, Asheville was the first town in North Carolina to outlaw the sale of liquor due directly to Will Harris' drunken massacre. This unpleasant event has not only had repercussions in the real world, but in the afterlife as well.

## The Haunts of the Barley's Area

Many believe the street where Barley's sits is haunted by the victims that were killed that day. Ghostly figures have been reported walking the streets at night and a policeman in an early 1900s uniform has been seen running down the street. Others have reported the sound of a howling dog and people screaming. The ghost of the dog killed has been allegedly been seen by several witnesses.

There are two other unique and interesting phantom sightings on the street near the pub. The first involves the spirits of spectral citizens seen walking past Barley's windows. This isn't that uncommon as far as ghost stories go, except that the windows where the spirits are seen rambling past are on the second floor! The second and more commonly reported spirit is that of a man seen in black clothes, from an earlier time, who walks towards the pub and disappears into thin air just as he reaches for the door. Another victim, perhaps of Will Harris, or the residual haunt of a bar regular, who like the character Norm on Cheers, came everyday? No one is certain.

The haunts associated with Barley's are not just in the street outside. Guests and staff at Barleys have reported hearing voices coming from empty rooms, phantom footsteps, and an elevator that works itself. Some have even reported seeing shadow figures within the building. There is even an apparition of a young woman seen repeatedly in the women's first floor restroom. Her presence is often indicated by the sudden and unexpectedly strong aroma of perfume.

Barley's is a regular on haunted pub crawls and a great place for catching live bluegrass, jazz, and friends. I have visited this Asheville haunt myself even inspecting the building, including the upstairs billiard room and the downstairs American Craft Beer area. I never experienced anything paranormal at Barley's myself. However, if you want a great slice of fresh sourdough pizza and a cold drink, you are definitely guaranteed that. I wish I could guarantee a paranormal experience but as I always say, ghosts don't perform on cue.

## NORTH CAROLINA
*Historic Haunts of the South III*

# THE DUNHILL'S PLAYFUL SPIRITS
*Dunhill Hotel, Charlotte, North Carolina*

Sometimes I find myself fascinated with attractive old buildings. Its even harder for me to not dig into the details of a place when I learn its haunted. This was the case with the Queens City's own Dunhill Hotel. This beautiful hotel intrigued me from the moment I spied its 10 story facade on North Tryon Street in the center of Charlotte's vibrant downtown arts and cultural area. Fortunately for me, while working on and collecting stories for this book, the gracious management of this historic Charlotte landmark agreed to share its history and ghostly tales and let me investigate for myself.

## The Story of the Dunhill

The Dunhill Hotel opened in November 1929 on the site where the Tryon Street Methodist Church once stood. It was built by doctors J.P. Matheson and C.N. Peeler and was designed by architect Louis Asbury Sr. It was 10 stories tall and opened with 100 rooms. Originally opened as the Mayfair Manor, the site of fabulously elegant apartment dwellings in downtown Charlotte. This neo classical beauty drew the attention of the wealthy citizens of Charlotte and a steady stream of businessmen traveling through by rail. Even the Great Depression and the building's conversion to a hotel couldn't douse the fiery excitement guests felt over its many unique amenities (for that time anyway). Guests were treated to electric dishwashers, their own bathrooms and radios and terrazo tile on the first and tenth floors. The Mayfair also featured upscale amenities like a restaurant, barber shop, and common area lounge with a fireplace where guests could gather with their friends.

J.P. Matheson died in 1937, but the hotel continued to operate until 1955. In 1959 the hotel sold to Dwight Phillips and it went through a $225,000 renovation and reopened in 1960 as the James Lee Motor Inn. Over subsequent years the hotel would suffer from mismanagement and failed investors culminating in its closing in 1981. It stood vacant until 1988. Squatters and the homeless took up residence in the empty building until it was purchased later in 1988 by the Dunhill Hotel Association. After $6 million of refurbishments and a parking garage being added, it opened once again, and this time as The Dunhill Hotel. It was soon after this, perhaps because of the stirring of spirits by the renovations, that word began to leak that the Dunhill was haunted.

## The Dunhill's Ghost Stories

The hotel has one particular ghost who comes up frequently in conversation and is affectionately known as "Dusty". Dusty is known to be friendly and many believe he may be the one to cause the elevator to randomly open on the upper and lower mezzanines on their own accord late at night. His spirit is a regular guest at the hotel.

Hotel staff often joke that Dusty has a girlfriend and that she is the one who haunts Room #505. For some unknown reason this room always smells like cocoa butter. The entire room has been refurbished, the current carpet, furniture, and decorations have

# NORTH CAROLINA
*The Dunhill's Playful Spirits*

all been changed numerous times and frequently laundered, yet the room still smells like cocoa butter. The hotel does not use cocoa butter to freshen or enhance the smell of any room, nor do they use it for any other purpose in the hotel. Of all the paranormal phenomenon to experience I can think of far worse than this.

When discussing phenomenon in the hotel, the third floor is brought up often. Many guests have experienced unusual things and "cold spots" thought to be tied to some kind of transient energies on the third floor. In fact, the third floor seems to be the coldest in the hotel. There was no special mention in these stories of a certain room that is affected more than the rest; it seems the entire floor suffers the lowered temperatures. Everyone at the Dunhill, staff and guests alike, report how cold it feels on this floor compared to the rest of the hotel.

Another area mentioned in many discussions of the building was the ninth floor, it has had a number of paranormal incidents. In fact, Room #906 is reported to be very active and haunted by a phantom house keeper. Guests often report hearing a rapping on the door at 3 a.m. and the disembodied word "Housekeeping!" spoken. Soon afterwards they describe feeling like a set of unseen hands tucking them in. The window blinds in this room are also known to open or close on their own as if trying to block out or let the light in depending upon the time of day.

## Possible Historical Reasons for the Haunts

The Dunhill building has seen a lot of history and while it has survived and in many cases thrived, it was not without incident. While most residents and guests enjoyed their time here during the Great Depression (when it was the Mayfair), victims of that time who saw their fortunes come and go have not been so happy. The hotel saw some suicides during this time. Further, during the renovations of the Dunhill before its opening, workers found pieces of a skull and bones in the basement in 1988. Police forensics experts analyzed the body parts and determined it to be the remains of an elderly man with a limp. It was suggested that he may have been one of the squatters or homeless there and may have fallen into the elevator shaft (or been pushed).

## Historic Haunts Investigates

When we arrived for our investigation in March 2015 we were happy to find ourselves staying in room #906. We checked in around 1pm. This left us time to set up the cameras in our room and explore the rest of the hotel and get base readings from our equipment throughout the hotel and in the other known hotspots.

Since it is supposed to be the coldest spot in the hotel, we decided to do temperature readings throughout the third floor. We discovered it to be a good ten degrees colder than the other

*The Dunhill in the heart of downtown Chrkotte*

# NORTH CAROLINA
*Historic Haunts of the South III*

parts of the hotel (except for the main level where cold air was coming in from the front and back exit doors). My husband Deric was able to explain away some of the mystery surrounding the third floor when he discovered the layout of the AC and air-handling system in the building. Much of it passes through the third floor area, and the ventilation in the kitchen area moves air quickly and strong enough that it can reportedly, drastically, cool or circulate the air in mere minutes (especially handy to remove smoke, extinguish fires, etc.) Still we did feel an eyebrow raising moment here.

We captured one set of strange spiked EMF readings, and that occurred when the elevator door closed unexpectedly on me on the third floor. Interestingly enough we were discussing the skeleton found at the bottom of the elevator shaft…and whether this could be the floor he fell from or was pushed at the time. The EMF spikes and the sudden unnaturally quick door closing happened at the exact moment we both came to the same suggestion and mentioned it out loud. We checked the elevator, but found no areas lacking insulation or places where elevator electronics might explain the EMF spikes. The elevator did not leave the floor to go to another, instead opening right back up slowly as normal.

After scouring the hotel with our equipment, doing base readings and interviews, and confirming the strong scent of Cocoa Butter around Room #505 (we couldn't go in it was occupied), we returned to our room. We noticed the blinds in our room had been manipulated. The house keeping staff had already been here and had left for the night. The digital recorder did pick up the sound, but the video camera was black. We had started it right as we exited the room and made sure it was recording normally. Later, once we returned home and reviewed the audio and video footage we learned that we did capture the sounds in the room, but nothing was caught on video.

While we didn't come away with a ton of evidence to categorically confirm it, we believe we have enough proof to say the Dunhill is haunted. Whether the haunts are caused by residual energy, intelligent energy or a little bit of both remains to be seen. Being at the Dunhill was an amazing experience and a place we hope to investigate again. One of Charlotte's few remaining historic landmarks, we thoroughly appreciated the elegant 18th century furnishings in our room, as well as the four-poster beds, hand made draperies, and the amazing food and hospitality. A regular part of the city's own ghost tours, it is a beautiful Historic Haunt in downtown Charlotte we look forward to returning to someday.

Parting Thought:

Just behind the hotel is Settler's Cemetery. The cemetery actually reaches past the walls and into the streets, and possibly underneath the parking garage as well. Maybe some of the backdoor neighbors come over to visit from time to time.

**NORTH CAROLINA**
*The Ghostly Writing's on the Wall, the Pub is Haunted*

# THE GHOSTLY WRITING'S ON THE WALL, THE PUB IS HAUNTED!

## Ri Ra's Irish Pub, Charlotte, North Carolina

*Ri Ra Irish Pub downtown Chrkotte*

I'm a feisty red headed Irish Girl! Or at least I've been told that occasionally especially by my husband and a few others. Having a strong Irish background, I feel a certain kinship to places touched by a "bit of the blarney". One such place was Ri Ra's Irish Pub on North Tryon Street. Stepping through the doors of this Charlotte Institution and favorite watering hole, is like being transported to another era. A split level beauty, Ri Ra's boasts several levels of bars with fabulous Irish music, food, antiquities and a ghost or two.

### The Story of Ri Ra's

The building now known as Ri Ra's Irish Pub in the middle of downtown Charlotte, was originally built as a department store. Some time after 1928 the store closed up shop. The structure remained an unremarkable piece of Charlotte until the 1990s when the building was purchased by two childhood friends from Ireland, David Kelly and Ciaran Sheehan, with the intent of building a unique Irish Pub. During construction of the pub, horse shoes and stable equipment were discovered suggesting that at some point the building was used as horse stables. Charlotte's "Ri Ra's" was the first to be built in a string of similarly named pubs and was opened in 1997.

The two friend's philosophy at the beginning was simple and one they've stuck with through the creation of this pub and others like it along the east coast and elsewhere (cities like Portland, Maine, Atlantic City, New Jersey, and Las Vegas, Nevada). Namely that all Ri Ra's are built with old wood from Ireland. If they don't have enough wood from old pubs, buildings, bars, etc. they will not build until they have gathered enough. Along the way they rescued artifacts, salvaged materials and many authentic parts (in whole or in segments) of true Irish bars. Many of these are hallmarks of Victorian Dublin.

For example, the Victorian bar in the middle of the pub was built in the early 1800s from the officer's mess in the Phoenix Barracks in Dublin. The bar was removed in the 1920s and kept in storage in Dublin for over 70 years. Sheehan bought the bar components in 1996 with an eye towards making it the centerpiece of his first location in Charlotte. To that end, he meticulously worked to restore it for the middle of the pub.

# NORTH CAROLINA
*Historic Haunts of the South III*

*Ri Ra interior including imported Irish storefront*

The city shop bar located at the front of the pub was acquired from a bar in Northern Ireland and dated from the 1740s. Another interesting piece in the pub is a statue of St. Patrick that is over 100 years old. Statues of this type were not uncommon in many rural towns and villages in Ireland and they were typically located at entrances to bless passers by, or in this case, the bar's customers.

Sections of the back bar include such unique conversation starters as a restored Guinness mirror and a collection of Dublin corporate ledgers from the early 1800s. The early 1800s is also the time frame of the etched glass panels set into the Victorian back-bar. These types of details make each Ri Ra's location unique, but in particular the first one here in Charlotte. Ri Ras would serve the community faithfully until 2009 when disaster struck this Publick House.

## The Fire

In May of 2009 a fire swept through the pub destroying much of its interior. For almost a year it remained closed as tireless efforts were being made to restore much of its interior. Fortunately, most of the original items and unique accents of the pub survived the blaze. The owners decided to take advantage of this time to restore, renovate, and make improvements, including the addition of hardwood parquet floor from Harland and Wolffe, the shipyards in Belfast where the Titanic was built. The bar reopened in 2010 to a flurry of activity by spirited customers and apparently, spirited ghosts.

## Ri Ra's Haunts

There are several active spirits here at RiRa's. In fact, according to the local walking Ghost Tour in Charlotte, an entire folder in the back room of this pub details paranormal incidents and investigations. Some have suggested the spirits could be Irish immigrants tied to the antiquities and pieces on display inside or former stable workers from its earlier incarnation.

The first spirit we learned of is a woman in a period dress seen walking throughout the building. She appears to be residual energy that moves throughout the building, but doesn't interact with anyone. You can't help but wonder what item, if any in the building, she might be attached to.

# NORTH CAROLINA
*The Ghostly Writing's on the Wall, the Pub is Haunted*

One of the other known spirits at Ri Ra's is a little girl in a white dress. She is reportedly periodically seen skipping and playing throughout the building before disappearing right before people's eyes. Some claim she is often seen with a piece of chalk in her hand and may be tied to the unique phenomenon upstairs.

## The Haunted Alphabet

Located on a small ledge on the second floor of the pub is a small desk and next to it a chalkboard area with the alphabet on it in chalk in a child's handwriting. According to employees this area should have been destroyed in the fire, but somehow miraculously and inexplicably survived. Employees tried to remove the alphabet many times and reportedly found they could not remove it on some occasions (even with cleaning solutions). On other occasions the writing would reappear the next day, in the same child's handwriting. To make this even more interesting, the ledge where the desk and chalkboard area are located is almost impossible for anyone to reach (especially after the fire) without a multi-story ladder. Yet the phenomenon still persists. Nowadays the letters are pointed out to the curious and mentioned in ghost tours along with stories of other activity at the pub.

## The Pub's Other Paranormal Activity

Employees of Ri Ra's have described cold spots in certain areas of the building. They've also described the appearance of various apparitions of men in period clothing seen walking around. Other apparitions have been seen by the staff, including that of a white dog. In short, active spots can be found in abundance throughout the pub. The spirits here have never reportedly tried to harm anyone, but Ri Ra's is worth visiting in hopes of some interaction (perhaps from the little girl's spirit.) Listen for her laughter and you may even see her skip by).

We have been to this unique Irish Pub on more than one occasion. Unfortunately, we have yet to experience the paranormal for ourselves (not that we would have noticed easily at the time as we were distracted by tasty food and a lively crowd). However, too many have had personal encounters, to not be at least a little curious. We hope to have a chance to investigate someday, perhaps when we come back to its fellow Historic Haunt across the street, the Dunhill Hotel. Even if the building wasn't inhabited by ghosts, it is definitely haunted by history…and spirits behind the bar.

## NORTH CAROLINA
*Historic Haunts of the South III*

# THE CORA TREE WITCH
*The Cora Tree, Brigands Bay, Frisco, North Carolina*

Its a witch! At least that's what the legend of the Cora Tree seems to be suggesting. If its to be believed it wouldn't be the first witch story I'd come across in my paranormal research (the Bell Witch - Historic Haunts of the South, the Fairfield Witch - Historic Haunts of the South II). This story definitely has a more supernatural slant than some of the others, but its well worth including.

### Cora's Story

In the early 1700s an unusual woman named Cora showed up in Frisco (then called Trent). She lived in a small dilapidated shack in the woods with her baby. She carried the baby everywhere and it seemed to be her only companion. Every time she arrived in town or showed up anywhere it was said that things would go wrong. If she touched a cow it supposedly went dry. A little boy is said to have made fun of her baby and he got so ill that he almost died. Fisherman at times wouldn't be able to catch any fish, but she would arrive and would catch all the fish she needed.

Stories began to surface around town that Cora had to be a witch. One day Captain Eli Blood arrived on his ship from Salem. Blood had heard the accusations and was curious whether Cora truly was a witch since he had heard the tales of misfortune as well.

Soon after Blood's arrival a young man's body washed ashore with a fearful expression upon his face, his hands linked as if he were praying for mercy and the number 666 was burned into his forehead. They also found tiny foot prints which they thought were a woman's, leading into the woods towards Cora's shack. That was all the justification the Captain needed.

### The Cora Tree Incident

Blood had Cora captured and the testing began to see if she really was a witch. She was tied up and thrown into the sound and she floated (she shouldn't have since she was weighted down). They even supposedly tried to cut her hair and it would not cut. Those were both said to be signs that she was a witch.

Cora was then taken to the live oak located on Snug Harbor Drive and tied to it holding her baby. Captain Tom Smith told Captain Blood he would not allow this execution to take place and that the Civil Courts should deal with it properly. According to legend it was at that moment that the baby then transformed into a cat with green eyes and ran off into the woods. Then suddenly from a clear sky there was a huge clap of thunder and as one in attendance wrote "there flashed a blinding bolt of lightning". The lightning hit the tree and the smoke was so thick that when it finally cleared Cora was gone and the word "CORA" was burned deep into the tree's trunk.

The tree is still there and has become a landmark. The legend is one of the more famous paranormal stories in all of the Carolinas. The curious travel to see the tree that still displays the name "CORA" burned into it. Some of these visitors have even reported the presence of a mysterious cat with glowing green eyes seen near the tree. Whether this phenomenon is a trick of reflective light in the eyes of a normal cat or the paranormal presence of Cora's "baby" remains to be seen. Visit the Cora Tree for yourself, and if you see the cat, decide for yourself.

## NORTH CAROLINA
Ghosts of the Lost Colony

# GHOSTS OF THE LOST COLONY
## The Lost Colony of Roanoke, Roanoke Island, North Carolina

As a paranormal investigator I often find myself dealing with mysteries and phenomenon. One of the biggest I have ever come across and one that to this day remains unanswered is the whereabouts of a small colony in what is today Dare County, North Carolina. This colony is of course the lost colony of Roanoke. While the claims of it being haunted have persisted for years, the mysteries surrounding its disappearance are just as haunting.

*All that remains of the lost colony*

### The Story of Roanoke

In the late 16th Century amidst bitter conflict at times with Spain, there was a desire on the part of Queen Elizabeth I to establish a permanent English settlement in the new world. To that end she agreed to a charter with Sir Walter Raleigh to help make the colony a reality. Raleigh worked with two men as his delegates Ralph Lane and Richard Grenville (one of his distant cousins).

Raleigh dispatched an exploratory expedition to the eastern coast of North America. They arrived ironically enough on July 4, 1584. They established relations with local natives the Secotans and Croatoans. Two Croatoans, Manteo and Wanchese returned to England and were able to give details about the geography and politics of the area. Based on this information Raleigh planned a second expedition to be led by Sir Richard Grenville.

This second expedition left with five ships in April of 1585. The ships got separated along the way, but reunited in the Outer Banks in early July 1585. During the first explorations of the mainland coast and native settlements, the settlers sacked and burned a native village because of a dispute over a silver cup. Despite this incident (and the bad blood it created), and a serious lack of food, Grenville decided to leave Ralph Lane and 107 men to establish a colony. He promised to return in April 1586 with fresh supplies and more men. A small fort was built and Grenville and his group departed in August of 1585.

April of 1586 came and went with no sign of Grenville. In June the colonists fought off an intense native attack. It was no surprise then that when Sir Francis Drake passed by on his way back to England and offered to give them a ride home they all

77

# NORTH CAROLINA
*Historic Haunts of the South III*

took him up on the offer. On the return trip they brought back with them tobacco, maize and potatoes. Grenville arrived shortly after Drake's departure and after finding an abandoned colony returned to England leaving only a small detachment to protect Raleigh's claim and maintain an English presence.

In July of 1587 Raleigh decided to send another expedition, a new group with 115 colonists including men ,women and children to establish a colony on Chesapeake Bay. The expedition was led by John White ( a friend of Raleigh's who would later be appointed Governor). They were ordered to stop along the way and check on the Roanoke contingent. They arrived on July 22, 1587 and found nothing except one skeleton believed to be one of the members of the English garrison. Once the lack of people had been discovered, the fleet's commander Simon Fernandez, for reasons unknown refused to let the colonists back on the ship to continue to Chesapeake Bay. He insisted instead that they establish the new colony on Roanoke.

John White began the process of setting up the colony and mending fences. He re-established relations with the Croatoans and local tribes, but those tribes that Ralph Lane had fought previously refused to meet with him. It was not long after this that colonist George Howe was killed by a native while he was scouring the area for crabs to eat. The colonists, understandably afraid, persuaded Governor White to make a return trip to England to plead their desperate need for help. White sailed for England late in 1587 leaving behind some seventeen women, eleven children, and ninety men. Among them White's daughter and her husband and Virginia Dare, the first English child born in the Americas, White's granddaughter.

Unfortunately for White, his plans for a quick trip back were thwarted. The Captain refused to sail in the winter. In addition, the coming of the Spanish Armada and the Anglo-Spanish War pulled every able-bodied English ship into the fight and left White no way to return to the colonists. White finally managed to gain passage on a privateering vessel with supplies. He landed at Roanoke on August 18, 1590, on his granddaughter's third birthday.

## The Lost Colony

Upon landing White discovered the settlement was deserted. He found no signs of struggle or battle. The people were gone,as were all the houses, cabins and shelters, all had been dismantled (which ruled out a speedy departure). He also found iron and other heavy objects in the heavy grass. The fort's fence posts, however, were still standing, and even more confusing were the words "Croatoan" carved in the fort's gate post and "Cro" etched in a tree nearby.

White had instructed the colonists to carve a Maltese Cross on a tree nearby , if they had been forced to flee or disappear, there was no cross. White thought perhaps the carving meant they had moved to "Croatoan Island", but couldn't continue the search with a storm forming and uncooperative men. The next day they left.

## So What Happened to the Colony

There seems to be five main theories as to the fate of the colony. First, some suggest that disease killed this group of settlers off. This is highly unlikely as their were no bodies or remnants and the houses had been dismantled. The second, and more

# NORTH CAROLINA
*Ghosts of the Lost Colony*

likely theory about Roanoke is that the people left the settlement, for the original location Chesapeake Bay, and may have built rafts or boats of some sort using the materials from the houses and structures in the settlement.

A similar theory is that the colonists moved fifty miles south to modern day Hatteras Island which at the time was known as Croatoan Island. This could be the reason they found "Croatoan" carved into the post of the gate at the fort to let others know they had moved south. A fourth scenario is that a hurricane or other severe storm hit and wiped out the village.However, had a storm of this nature hit its extremely unlikely to have wiped out all remnants of the colony's buildings and structures while leaving the surrounding fence untouched. The fifth and highly likely scenario suggests that the colonists were attacked and killed by the native Americans, and that the buildings and structures were dismantled afterward. Later encounters would seem to point to this possibility.

## In the Aftermath

Raleigh attempted to discover the colonies whereabouts, in 1602 he had his own boat and paid crew (paid to avoid pirateering distractions). Shortly after landing in the Outer Banks, however, bad weather forced them to turn around and leave without ever making it to Roanoke Island. Raleigh was arrested for treason shortly after this and unable to send any other missions.

Later in 1608, Captain John Smith (of Pocahontas fame) was tasked with discovering what happened to the settlers of Roanoke. He learned that the chief of the Powhatan tribe claimed to have personally conducted the slaughter of the lost colonists, prior to his arrival. He produced English made iron items as proof. Rumors of survivors of the slaughter persisted and several search expeditions were mounted, but no trace of the lost colony was found. Recent evidence, however, suggests that the slaughter (if there was one) had nothing to do with the lost colony.

In 1612 word got to England that William Strachey, Secretary of Jamestown, had taken note of a few unusual things. Some Indian settlements had two story homes with stone walls, He also discussed the discovery of Englishmen on site, four boys and one girl sighted at an Eno Indian settlement. These captives were forced to beat copper. It was speculated that the girl could have been Virginia Dare.

The possibility of surviving settlers is also suggested by several writers and explorers throughout the 17th and 18th centuries. These writers describe encounters with Indians who claim descent from Roanoke colonists and had strikingly European features. In addition, the Indian's vocabulary included several obsolete English phrases.

## The Haunts of Roanoke

Many who have visited The Lost Colony of Roanoke have experienced and reported paranormal activity. Reports including the sensation of being watched from the woods are extremely common, as are footsteps and the sounds of rustling leaves and cracking branches with no winds or animals visible to explain it. Others have claimed to have actually seen people in 16th century attire or Native Americans in the area (and not the performers or re-enactors).

# NORTH CAROLINA
*Historic Haunts of the South III*

I visited here with a group in 2012 We experienced the sensation of unseen eyes peering at us as we walked through the area and down the paths. The entire time, someone seemed to be following us. At times we even heard the footsteps and kept turning expecting to see another tourist, but in every case, we were alone.

Roanoke Island has frequent reports of paranormal activity of a more unusual kind as well. The ghostly spirit of a bright white deer has been encountered many times near the site of the lost colony. Native Americans claim the deer is the spirit of Virginia Dare and suggest another explanation for the missing colonists. Croatoans believed that Roanoke Island had a spirit and if angered this spirit had the power to change those who angered it into the forms of rocks, trees and animals. These indian stories suggest the idea that all the colonists were transformed including young Virginia Dare (hence the white deer).

If you ever find yourself in this part of the Carolinas make sure to explore the site of the lost colony. Whether you experience a phantom settler, indian, or other paranormal entity or not, it doesn't really matter. This area is so haunted with history you can't go wrong. This is one of my favorite Historic Haunts in the Outer Banks of North Carolina.

Parting Mention:

The Mysterious Significance of CROATOAN

"CROATOAN" as carved in the post at Roanoke has developed something of a supernatural quality itself. It has appeared numerous times in North America in the last few centuries, in most cases not even close to the Carolinas. Edgar Allen Poe after an unexplained disappearance and a few days before his death was whispering "CROATOAN" while in a state of delirium. The word was also found scribbled in the journal of Amelia Earhart after her disappearance in 1937.

CROATOAN was carved in the bedpost of the bed slept in by celebrated horror author Ambrose Bierce before he vanished in Mexico in 1913. The word was written on the last page of the logbook of the ship Carrol A. Deering before it ran aground with no one on board on Cape Hatteras in 1921 (not far from what was known as Croatoan Island)

SOUTH CAROLINA

# REVOLUTIONARY SPIRITS OF KINGS MOUNTAIN

Kings Mountain National Military Park, Blacksburg, SC

Sometimes what seems like a fleeting moment in history can have profound repercussions. This was definitely the case at the North Carolina/South Carolina border at King's Mountain. It was there that General Nathaniel Greene and his Overmountain men defeated the British and American loyalist forces in a mere sixty five minutes and made historic steps toward American Independence.

### A Bit More About Kings Mountain

Thomas Jefferson commented on the Battle of Kings Mountain, considering it "The turn of the tide of success". On October 7th, 1780 the battle destroyed the left wing of Lord Cornwallis' Army ending the loyalist ascendance in the Carolinas. It halted the British advances into North Carolina and forced Cornwallis to retreat in just a little over an hour. It was a very short event but a successful one.

*Kings Mountain Marker*

During the skirmish the British sustained approximately 244 casualties including the death of Major Patrick Ferguson who led them into battle.

Today Major Ferguson is recognized, his gravesite is among the historic sites at this National Military Park. As an important battle site and possible turning point of the Revolutionary War it has been recognized on the National Register of Historic Places as of 1996. Kings Mountain National Military Park commemorates an important chapter in our history and the men who fought and died here. Some of these men, at least in spirit, remain.

### The Ghosts of Kings Mountain

Major Ferguson's ghost is often seen near the location where he is buried at Kings Mountain National Military Park. Many believe his apparition is encountered because he did not receive a respectful burial. It is said that Major Ferguson was stripped and urinated on by Patriot soldiers before being buried beneath a pile of stones. Staff members who work for the park, visitors, and reenactors have all claimed to have seen the General in his uniform at the park. They feel a little uneasy when they have witnessed his ghost walking near his burial site or peering at them from the shadows.

# SOUTH CAROLINA
*Historic Haunts of the South III*

Ferguson's ghost is not alone. Other apparitions have been reported including men on horseback in Revolutionary era garb seen riding through the park before vanishing. The phantom sounds of battle have often been reported as have a variety of other paranormal activity. Among these are disembodied voices, screams, phantom knocks, light anomalies, electrical disturbances and reports by many who felt like they were being watched.

## My Experiences

While here in 2009, I too felt I was being watched from the woods the entire time I was there. And I wasn't the only one. Several others kept turning around to see who was behind them. We compared notes and the other visitors had the same weary sensation I did. The park gets these and other reports of paranormal activity on a regular basis and they think of it as a common day to day occurrence here. If you're a fan of history or the paranormal like me, make sure to check out this historic site and perhaps the haunts will seek you out as well.

# DRAYTON'S HAUNT THE HALL
*Drayton Hall, Charleston, South Carolina*

Drayton Hall sits on the beautiful Ashley River in Charleston South Carolina. It has survived the Revolutionary War and the Civil War. Unlike other Charleston area plantations, this building and its beautiful detail and plasterwork survived when other plantations were destroyed. Perhaps that's due to the reported family spirits still keeping an eye on the hall as they have throughout its long history.

*Drayton Hall*

## Drayton Hall's History

It was built by John Drayton who bought the property in the 1730s and built his home between 1747 and 1752. His parents owned Magnolia Plantation (featured in Historic Haunts of the South II) where he grew up. While his father had been mainly a rancher, John Drayton made the transition from rancher to planter. The main crop for Drayton Hall was indigo and rice and this is where Drayton made his money.

Drayton enjoyed great success until the coming of the British. They first came in 1779, but returned in force in 1780. Learning that they were coming ahead of time, John and his family packed early and left before the British arrived. Unfortunately, John Drayton died while crossing the Cooper River and was buried in an unmarked grave.

Drayton Hall would become the headquarters for British Commander Sir Henry Clinton, and after a base of operations for the British to lay siege to Charleston. Later British General Charles Cornwallis took over the house and grounds with his forces. In 1782, American General "Mad" Anthony Wayne headquartered here until the British evacuated.

Charles Drayton (John's son) took over the house after the Revolutionary War and was elected Lt. Governor in 1785. He cultivated indigo and cotton on the plantation and managed the house. He was forced to make some changes to the Drayton estate after a hurricane, but during his life he did his best to care for the building and grounds and when he passed he handed it down to members of the family.

During the Civil War Drayton plantation survived when other antebellum plantations were burned or destroyed by serving as a hospital (or as some accounts claim, pretending to do so). The Drayton family also had to change crops and customers as the war disrupted supply lines, shipping channels and contacts. The plantation survived and the family legacy continued. In all seven generations of Draytons lived, worked, and died here.

# SOUTH CAROLINA
*Historic Haunts of the South III*

In 1886 an earthquake destroyed the laundry house, thankfully nothing more, and in 1893 a hurricane destroyed the kitchen. Still the family and site endured. In fact, the house saw Drayton family ownership or occupation until it was sold to the National Trust for Historic Preservation in 1974. Along the way the family kept Drayton Hall in its former state, resisting the urge to update to modern conveniences and amenities. The Draytons lived here a long time and some of them reportedly still do...in spirit anyway.

## Drayton's Haunts

If you discuss the topic of spirits residing in this beautiful plantation home with someone in the area you'll quickly learn it depends on who you talk to. Some say there are no ghosts here; others say the place is packed. Fortunately, we have enough paranormal reports to reference to lean towards the latter.

Some of the paranormal reports from Drayton state that some of the slaves ghosts have remained here and are still continuing on with their duties (residual haunts it seems). Others believe that some of the Draytons are still here overseeing their plantation. Indeed William Henry Drayton is said to haunt the Hall and it was featured on America's Most Haunted Places.

## Historic Haunts Visits

Whether the consensus on the building is that its haunted or not, while visiting here doing my research in 2012, I felt a very strong male presence in the main house. It wasn't negative or threatening in anyway. It just felt as if the man of the house was home and keeping a watchful eye on things. We also heard a door close right behind us, but when we turned no one was there and the door had been shut. We tested it out and there was no way it would have just swung shut on its own and there was no gust of air or other easy and obvious explanation

This is one of my favorite Historic Haunts outside of the downtown Charleston area along with its sister plantation, Magnolia. The house remains in its pure state and gives us a glimpse into the daily life of the time. I find the house and its interiors to be beautiful and I was happy to include it in this book.

# THE FRIENDLY AND CURIOUS GHOSTS OF THE LODGE ALLEY INN

*Lodge Alley Inn, Charleston, South Carolina*

*The Lodge Alley Inn*

Sometimes in my travels I find myself just as taken by a beautiful place to stay as I do by the ghost stories that involve it. This was the case with the Lodge Alley Inn, a remarkable collection of Victorian style suites nestled in the heart of downtown Charleston. When my husband and I arrived we were originally only here to do a booksigning in town and visit some good friends. When we checked in and learned the place was haunted we were thankful we grabbed some of our equipment before leaving and began planning an impromptu investigation in the elevator on the way up to our room (this kind of good luck doesn't happen often so you gotta be ready on the fly sometimes). When we arrived in our room and began to unpack and work out the details for the investigation we were both blown away by the old world charm and new world amenities of our room and the Inn. How could you not be attracted to the four-poster beds, spiral staircases, original pine floors, red brick walls and thick oriental carpets. As I marveled at the huge loft spaces, street view of downtown Charleston out our window, fireplace and other room details, my husband smiled and said, "I know, and what's even better is the fact that its a Historic Haunt and we get to investigate."

# SOUTH CAROLINA
*Historic Haunts of the South III*

## Looking Back at the Lodge Alley's Past

This 18th century collection of fifteen warehouses was named after a ten foot wide alley that adjoins the buildings and is paved by Belgian block bricks. The alley was built so people on State Street could have a shortcut from their homes or businesses straight to the docks were the ships were loaded. The Lodge of Freemasons first established the alley in 1773 on a site where French Huguenots once had their warehouses and dwellings.

During the American Revolution (one of my favorite times of our history) the Liberty Boys met at the warehouse and plotted their own version of the Boston Tea Party. They did so by forcing Charleston merchants who had ordered several chests of taxed British tea to toss it into Charleston Harbor to prove a point to England. This was actually Charleston's second "tea party", the first preceded Boston's by thirteen days.

Many of the taverns, homes, carriage houses, and other warehouses near the harbor were destroyed throughout the years by the tragic disasters Charleston faced. Fires, hurricanes, and tornadoes had a devastating effect and claimed much of the early historic areas. However, the now Lodge Alley Inn survived through these catastrophes and for a time thrived.

The Lodge Alley Inn warehouses were in danger of being leveled by a developer intent on building skyscrapers until the Save Charleston Foundation bought and began restoring the warehouses. The buildings went through the major renovations and opened in 1983 as the Lodge Alley Inn. It is part of the Bluegreen Resort family. The property now consists of over fifteen separate warehouse buildings that make up this beautiful complex. Needless to say with the age and history of the building, there are a few ghost stories to tell.

## The Lodge Alley Hauntings

While staying here for a couple of nights in June 2014 during a series of book signings at the Old Exchange and Provost Dungeon (which was featured in Historic Haunts of the South) we heard a few of the ghostly encounters the staff and guests have had. They were very cooperative. They made it easy to squeeze in this surprise investigation and gather as many details as we could.

It seems most of the accounts of paranormal activity came from the third floor of the main building. We chatted at length with one of the valets and he shared some of his personal experiences. He told us that during his first encounter he was taking care of something on the third floor. While walking towards the vending machines he felt something behind him, but when he turned no one was there. When he continued on and approached the vending machine he saw a shadow of someone behind him in the window of the machine and felt a breath on the back of his neck. He began to turn around and saw the entity, it was a smoky shadow figure that faded to mist then disappeared. Needless to say this startled him a bit and he went to the front desk to share the encounter with another staff member. They replied with, "Oh! You too?" Apparently this type of activity is not uncommon.

He went on to tell us that the house keeping staff has also experienced this on numerous occasions on the third floor as well. Misty forms, shadows, and breaths on

# SOUTH CAROLINA

*The Friendly and Curious Ghosts of the Lodge Alley Inn*

the back of the neck occur on a regular basis. We were staying in Room #208 on the second floor, but had to make our way up to the third floor to see for ourselves. We checked everything out thoroughly. We did have some random K2 spikes and Mel Meter readings, but as far as ghostly apparitions, we didn't encounter anything. However, the air did seem a little heavier on the third floor than it did on the second floor.

In addition to the staff, plenty of guests have had unusual experiences at the Inn, at the splendid courtyard outside, the High Cotton restaurant next door (a delicious Award Winning treat) and in the resort building itself. Guests on the third floor have even checked out in the middle of the night due to the racket coming from above them. Some have said it sounds like a party is taking place above their heads or someone is moving furniture. Funny thing is, for the most part there are no guest rooms above the heads of the guests who complained. A few of the warehouse buildings feature a small storage space or a one room daytime office space but most of the buildings have no fourth floor!

We were happy to discover that whoever or whatever is here isn't malevolent, just curious to discover who is here and what is going on. Guests who have encountered spirits first hand have described them as friendly, curious and happy to visit. The building interiors, after their beautiful transformations from warehouse space to Victorian-style interiors look nothing like they once did. If the spirits here are from another era, I'm sure it is quite confusing to them. I hope we get to go back and do a proper investigation and grab a few more of the complimentary fresh-baked cookies.

## SOUTH CAROLINA
*Historic Haunts of the South III*

# THE GHOSTS OF RUINS AND RIDERS
## Old Sheldon Church Ruins, Yemassee, South Carolina

*The Old Sheldon Church Ruins*

I love when I accidentally stumble across a beautiful or unknown (to me) historic site that turns out to be haunted. This was the case not too long ago when my husband and I were returning from a weekend of paranormal investigating and researching in South Carolina. We were driving back to Florida from Charleston, and decided to stop at the roadside store, Carolina Pie, to pick up a few things. While there we inquired about a picture we saw on a postcard and learned of the Old Sheldon Church Ruins. One of the women behind the counter got wide eyed when we asked if they knew of any ghosts. She shared the location of the nearby ruins and a tale or two about it.

### The Story of the Ruins

On a historic site in northern Beaufort County lies the ruins of old Sheldon Church. The preexisting building was originally known as Prince William's Parish Church. It was built between 1745 and 1753 and was built in the style of the Greek revival. The church was burned in 1779 by the British and General Provost during the Revolutionary War, but because of its masterful construction, most of the brick structure withstood the fire.

The church interior was rebuilt in 1826, but was burned again in 1865 when Union General Sherman marched from Georgia into South Carolina during the Civil War. While it was originally thought that the bulk of the inside of the church had burned during Sherman's march, recent evidence would suggest otherwise. Old letters from records in the area suggest that the church's interior may have been gutted and the materials reused to rebuild the homes destroyed by Sherman.

In addition to the surviving remnants of this historic structure that endured the General's march, there is a rather important grave inside the church. The grave is that of Colonel William Bull who assisted General Oglethorpe in designing the layout of Savannah. Bull surveyed the land and formed the grid pattern of the streets and squares.

Among the majestic gnarled oaks and spanish moss are other scattered graves and stones. These historic ruins and their surroundings have been placed on the National Historic Register. They have proven to be a popular Low Country spot for weddings, photographs, tourism and apparently ghost spotting.

## Spirits of the Old Church Ruins

The first ghostly tale we came across involving the old church came from the employees of the Carolina Pie Store. One of the helpful women there told us that one night a friend of hers, picked up a person needing a lift who said they wanted to be dropped off at the old church. When the driver stopped to let the rider out, the passenger vanished. Doing a little more digging, we learned that this incident has happened more than once to others. In every case the ghostly passenger always asks to be dropped off at the church then disappears once they arrive.

The paranormal tales involving the church are not limited to a phantom rider, however. Visitors alone at the old church ruins have reported hearing heavy footsteps in the grass despite being the only ones present. Paranormal groups have investigated the site and have captured activity. Other witnesses have described the appearance of unexplainable flashing lights.

Perhaps the most interesting of the paranormal occurrences centers around the apparition of a young woman. This ghost has been seen several times and has been reportedly encountered wearing a simple brown dress standing over a baby's grave. Visitors who walk near the child's tombstone sometimes feel an overwhelming sense of sorrow.

We may never find out who the young woman is, but we know one thing, the Old Sheldon Church Ruins are a beautiful and peaceful spot to enjoy history, nature, and a picnic. Be mindful though if you see someone looking for a ride on the way there. A helpful gesture may turn into a ghostly encounter at this Historic Haunt.

TENNESSEE

# THE GHOSTS OF CHICKAMAUGA
*Chickamauga Battlefield, Chattanooga, Tennessee*

During the fall of 1863, Union and Confederate soldiers met in conflict in north Georgia and southeastern Tennessee. Their eyes were set on Chattanooga and it was one of the toughest battles of the Civil War. Chattanooga was the key to the railroad and it would be a grand prize for whoever could take it.

Union General William S. Rosecrans forced Confederate General Braxton Bragg and his men to withdraw from middle Tennessee to Chattanooga. The fighting started on September 19th and the Union also tried to keep supplies from the Rebels. When General Ulysses S. Grant took overall command over northern forces everything changed after a series of battles and a charge up Lookout Mountain. The Union did eventually win the battle and took control over the city and most of Tennessee. There were 34,624 casualties total (16,170 Union and 18,454 Confederate). Eventually of course the North would go on to win the war.

After the Civil War the area was used as a training center for troops during the Spanish American War. When that war ended, efforts were made (and spearheaded by former Union Generals) to establish a military park to commemorate the events made famous on the site and the men who gave their lives in service. The National Park Service runs the area today and in 1966 it was added to the National Register of Historic Places. The site is full of history and apparently, full of ghosts.

*Glowing Green Eyes*

Glowing green eyes are often seen on foggy days at the battlefield and have been reported since before the battle took place, for over 200 years. Some believe the green eyes are from a soldier that was killed during battle on horseback and it is actually the horse's eyes that are seen. Reports of the apparition of a horse with glowing eyes with a soldier on his back seem to be a common occurrence on foggy days.

During the War of 1812 approximately 500 Cherokee Indians fought with General Andrew Jackson against the Creek Indians in this same area. Many locals believe the Indians who died in that battle are still here. It has been suggested that maybe the glowing green eyes are actually from that battle instead of the one fought during the Civil War.

I have to admit, during foggy mornings or during storms this area can feel a bit eerie and you can easily creep yourself out. I have never seen the green glowing eyes or the soldier upon the horse, but the area does give off a very strong impression that makes you feel like unseen eyes are watching you.

It is an amazing piece of Civil War history and definitely one of our favorite Tennessee Historic Haunts.

# HURRICANE MILLS: THE HAUNTS OF LORETTA LYNN'S PLACE

*Loretta Lynn's Plantation, Hurricane Mills, Tennessee*

Loretta Webb was born on April 14th, 1932 in Kentucky. At the age of 14/15 this "Coal Miner's Daughter" married 21 year old Oliver Vanetta Lynn. They had six children early on and were married for almost 50 rocky years before his death. In 1953 her husband bought her a guitar and she taught herself how to play. She worked her way through small bar gigs and performances, with her sights set on Nashville. She hit the country music scene in Nashville in the 1960s with a vengeance. She eventually had sixteen #1 hits and seventy charted songs as a solo artist and duet partner. She is considered "The First Lady of Country Music".

## Loretta's Place

Loretta Lynn's Plantation in Hurricane Mills is said to be the "seventh largest attraction in Tennessee" and includes a recording studio, museum, and much more. Many people go here every year to see this great country artist's home and momentos from her career. Others come in search of the spirits who allegedly haunt this plantation.

## The Haunts of Hurricane Mills

After the Lynn family moved here in 1966 stories began to circulate about the property being haunted. The Lynn family had experiences for themselves as have staff and guests through the years. While some of the most intense experiences happened in the house itself, the paranormal activity on the grounds has been substantial as well and is worth mentioning.

There is a woman in white who roams the grounds. Her name is Beula Anderson. It was chronicled that her newborn baby son died and twelve days after his death she too died from grief. For decades many have reported seeing her apparition all dressed in white crying, apparently still grieving the loss of her son. This ghost has also been seen at nearby Anderson cemetery where she and her son are buried.

Beula isn't the only spirit still haunting the grounds. Two Civil War soldiers have also been seen. Not long after settling in and discovering the paranormally active property, Loretta learned there was a Civil War battle once fought on the property and that nineteen Confederate Soldiers are buried there. A "slave pit" from the same era was also once located on property and the disembodied sounds of dragging chains and other unusual activity have often been mentioned. In fact, strange occurrences have been reported here for decades and it seems like the more you visit there or the longer you stay, the more apt you are to see things.

## Haunts of the House Itself

The Lynn family's paranormal experiences have been documented before and weren't limited to the grounds of the property. Soon after they moved in unusual things began to happen. Loretta noticed that no matter how often she straightened the pictures in the house they always ended up crooked again. She also noticed the door between her room and her twin daughters would open and close by itself. Her twin girls described seeing the apparitions in their bedroom of women with their hair swept up in old fashioned clothing. Her oldest son was surprised by the sudden ethereal presence of a Civil War Soldier at the foot of his bed.

Loretta has been known to be something of a "sensitive" when it comes to spirits and the afterlife, and she never shies away from discussing it. She saw the ghost of her departed father in the house she grew up in. She has also reportedly made contact with an angry spirit named Anderson. When she researched the name she learned that James Anderson was a former owner of the house and buried nearby.

Over ten years ago this location was featured on a paranormal television show and ever since then it has been on my list of places to see. Not because I am a country music fan, I'm not, however, I have a tremendous respect for Loretta Lynn and all that she's accomplished. I also have a healthy respect for places with this much paranormal activity. I hope to visit this Historic Haunt myself one day and dig deeper into its interesting history and haunted tales.

## VIRGINIA

# THE BRAVE GHOSTS OF THE BRAFFERTON
*The Brafferton Building,*
*College of William and Mary, Williamsburg, Virginia*

As I've mentioned before I'm a huge fan of the College of William and Mary in Williamsburg, Virginia. The college and surrounding areas are a treasure trove of historical and colonial era buildings. The second oldest on campus and one of the most notorious is the Brafferton Building. Brafferton's connection to education is obvious in its capacity as offices for staff of the school, but many are in the dark about the building's less than savory past and the ghosts that still haunt this area.

*William and Mary's Brafferton Building*

### The Brafferton's Founding and Its Unhappy Students

The Brafferton Building is part of the College of William and Mary and was built in 1723 just east of the Wren Building. Funding for the building was provided by the English naturalist philosopher Robert Boyle. Under it's charter it was built with the intent to teach Indian boys english and provide them with an education so they could later spread the Gospel to the Indian tribes. Unfortunately, many of the young Indian children who passed through those halls and slept in the rooms came here in the worst possible ways. A majority were forcibly removed from their families and brought here against their wills. In some cases, their fathers were killed before they were taken to be "educated" at the school.

After a time, the school's headmaster died, leaving a house full of unhappy boys. Most of the boys came from different tribes and spoke different languages making communication near impossible. Further, severe conditions and discipline, as well as meager food and sanitation, led to many of the boys being malnourished, falling ill and in some cases dying. Lonely and desperate others reportedly attempted to escape at night, but were surrounded and outnumbered by townsfolk who didn't like them and cared little for their plight. After several escape attempts the boys were reportedly locked in at night. The "Indian" school eventually closed in 1779. Today it serves the college as offices and a reminder of a well intentioned idea gone terribly wrong.

# VIRGINIA
*Historic Haunts of the South III*

## The Brave Spirits at the Brafferton

Many believe the building is haunted by the young boys who passed away. People have reported footsteps in the halls, the sounds of inaudible voices, and sobbing and moaning. There have even been frequent reports of Indian drums or Tom Toms.

Perhaps the biggest and most often reported encounters with these spirits is at night. Especially foggy nights lit only by the moon light. Dozens of reports state people seeing the apparitions of young male Indians running across the lawn in front of the Brafferton and the Wren Buildings. They are seen running the length of the Sunken Garden behind the Wren. In most cases these reported spirits of young Indian boys are seen bare-chested and barefooted. Some have suggested that they could be residual haunts still trying to escape from the building and their unfortunate circumstances.

## My Time Here and Thoughts

I have never seen these apparitions, but on foggy moonlit nights the College does take on a completely different feel and I know this from experience. When on campus at night, you sometimes feel as if unseen eyes are upon you. That doesn't mean anything here is malicious, but it can make you feel a bit creepy.

The ghosts of the young Indian boys are seen so often they are a part of student lore. They are mentioned in ghost stories of the campus. If you want to hear more ghostly tales from the College of William and Mary, be sure to check out the 4th book in my Historic Haunts series, the South 2.

## VIRGINIA
An Amorous Apparition at the Brick House Taven

# AN AMOROUS APPARITION AT THE BRICK HOUSE TAVERN

Brick House Tavern and Shop, Colonial Williamsburg, Virginia

*Brick House Tavern*

The Brick House Tavern Guest House in Colonial Williamsburg is one of the more popular guest houses available to rent by the public. Visitors appreciate the convenience and proximity this Duke of Gloucester Street landmark provides to the other attractions at Colonial Williamsburg. However, its not the first "Brick House Tavern" to have been built here. According to a historical report filed in the digital library of Colonial Williamsburg, the first was an...

"Eighty foot brick house having complete cellars underneath, four separate entrances and about fourteen lodging rooms..." which "...stood on the corner of Botetourt and Duke of Gloucester Street until it was destroyed by a disastrous fire in April 1842, which burned practically every brick in that block."

Fortunately, surviving floor plans, drawn to scale in considerable detail, and the almost intact original foundations made accurate reconstruction possible in 1939. The hand made and fired bricks (as in colonial days) helped builders achieve the utmost in authenticity. Surviving records also gave us a pretty good look at the original building and what life was like back then.

### The Brick House and Shop History

The original buildings are believed to date from sometime prior to 1723. A gentleman named Dudley Digges leased lots for private shops or tenements. A wig maker had leased the spot where the shop stood. Digges sold the lots to William Withers, a merchant who was also the private secretary of the Royal Governor. By that time the tavern had already been in operation for almost fifty years and was occupied by tavernkeeper Mrs. Christianne Campbell. It was sold again in 1760 to another merchant, William Holt, for 350 Pounds. Holt would turn around and sell the property again in March of the next year.

In 1761 Dr. William Carter (surgeon, apothecary, and businessman) purchased a building for 375 pounds. By then it was already known as Williamsburg's first "office" building with six doors on the front and six on the back courtyard. Carter thought it ideally suited for business.

In 1770, the same building known as the Brick House Tavern with Mary Davis as the innkeeper, advertised ..."12 or 14 very good lodging rooms with fireplaces in most

95

# VIRGINIA
*Historic Haunts of the South III*

of them." The rooms on the first floor were for the lady guests and the ones on the second floor were for the gentlemen. Even then the inn was busy.

Staying in an Inn was much different back then than the 16 private rooms with full baths enjoyed at the Brick House today. A "standard price" room for the night entitled you to a place to sleep and a meal, but this place to sleep was a bed shared with perfect strangers and housing as many as 20 people. If you were fortunate enough to afford "private accommodations" you slept alone in your own bed, but several beds were still located in the same room. This was normal for many Inns of the time and the Brick House thrived. In fact, it was still in business at the end of the War of 1812 because it is documented that American Cavalry troops found lodging here at that time. There was even evidence of remaining Inn segments as late as the Civil War.

## Spirits at the Brick House Tavern and Shop

Shortly after the Brick House Tavern and Shop rebuilt on the old foundations and provided as it's old sign proclaimed "Guest Rooms for Ladies and Gentlemen", stories of the paranormal emerged. These reports persist to this day and include a variety of unusual activity including reports of unnerving sleep paralysis, phantom odors of sweat and tobacco (in a non-smoking building), disembodied noises of jangling keys, reports of shadow figures, and lights and faucets mysteriously turned on and off. Further, at least one female guest reported the sobering tale of an intelligent haunt dressed in plaid that drew her sympathies until he tried to lean in and kiss her before disappearing into thin air.

## Our Experience at the Brick House

In May 2015 one of my investigative team members, Amy Mann, and I traveled to Colonial Williamsburg for a mini "girls trip". We never leave home without some paranormal equipment on us. This proved useful because when we arrived, we experienced something on the very first night!

We were climbing the stairs to go up to our room and we heard footsteps following us. We moved to the right because we thought someone was behind us trying to pass, but when we did this, the footsteps stopped shortly thereafter and there was no one there with us. This happened to us on several occasions during our stay and we started joking about our phantom footfalls every time either one of us encountered it. Wanting to make sure we did our due diligence as investigators we did check for any temperature or EMF fluctuations on the stairs and the base EMF was 0 and the temperature was always the same. We also ruled out echoes and other possible causes for the footsteps.

Going over the little evidence we seemed to have on this investigation we reasoned that perhaps what we experienced was just residual energy of a past innkeeper or guest or maybe even the good doctor. Regardless of what caused the activity, we did enjoy staying there and will be back hopefully to investigate again and gather more evidence. Besides, Williamsburg will always be home to me and to some of my favorite Historic Haunts.

# VIRGINIA
The Phantom Music of Bruton Parish Church

# THE PHANTOM MUSIC OF BRUTON PARISH CHURCH

Bruton Parish Church, Colonial Williamsburg, VA

As fans of my Historic Haunts books have no doubt learned by now I am a big supporter of Colonial Williamsburg. The place is full of history and connections to the founding of our country. It's also full of ghost stories and haunted locations many of which I've discussed (Historic Haunts of the South I + II) and some still left to discover. One of those is Bruton Parish Church.

*Bruton Parish Church*

## Bruton Parish's Past

Bruton Parish Church was the First Anglican Church in Williamsburg Virginia in 1660 when the town was still known as Middle Plantation. The current structure seen today is the third church. The first building was located most likely in the fields and in 1677 the vestry ordered a brick structure built in town on land that was donated by John Page. The second church was finished by November 1683 but was destroyed by fire. The foundation is still visible just north of the current structure which was completed in 1715. Some of the great minds of the Revolutionary War attended this church including; Thomas Jefferson, George Washington, Patrick Henry, Richard Henry Lee, and George Wythe, among many others (including my 8th, 9th, and 10th great grandparents).

Many who tour or attend this beautiful church today wonder who the grand canopied chair upon the platform was for. In 1716, Governor Spotswood attended services in that chair. In 1718 a gallery was added to the church for students of the College of William and Mary. Another interesting tidbit about this church is that back in Colonial days, men and woman did not sit together. Here the men sat on the north side and the woman sat on the south.

In 1761 the church was presented with a church bell by James Tarpley, a local merchant. It became famous as Virginia's "Liberty Bell" ringing in celebration of the Declaration of Independence some seven years later. The church (and its bell) played a central role to its congregation, the nearby College of William and Mary, and its community. During the Battle of Yorktown in 1781 and the Battle of Williamsburg in 1862, the church served as a hospital.

Moving several years forward to 1903, the great Reverend Dr. W.A.R. Goodwin became rector of Bruton Parish Church and began an amazing restoration project on

# VIRGINIA
*Historic Haunts of the South III*

the church. This project would later spread throughout the town and lead to the restoration, re-creation or re-imagining of Colonial Williamsburg by Goodwin among others and of course the generous funding and support of the Rockefeller family. The church was dedicated in 1907 and is the beautiful house of worship you see today. It is quickly approaching the 300 year mark of service and guidance to its attendees and the town of Colonial Williamsburg.

I have a strong passion for this church because I did attend it when I lived in Williamsburg. Its history is rich and historic. Not only do I find that intriguing, but I've been told of more than one experience with the paranormal here and I've had a few myself.

## The Paranormal at Bruton Parish

Back during the colonial days, Peter Pelham (the gaol keeper) was also the organist at the church. On many occasions late at night when the town is quiet and most are in bed, I would take a stroll down Duke of Gloucester Street and would often hear organ music. The church at the time would be closed, locked, and completely empty, but you could still hear the ethereal sounds of the organ being played. It has such a beautiful and distinct sound and I was not the only one who experienced this phenomenon. Several other members of the Historic Haunts Investigations team have experienced this as well. I also have many friends who work for Colonial Williamsburg and they have experienced this phenomenon for themselves, They've even gone into the church during several of these episodes whereupon the music instantly ceased and they found the building empty.

Many believe the phantom organist is Mr. Pelham himself still practicing for Sunday service. He also reportedly still keeps watch over the Public Gaol ( if you want to hear more about that, check out Historic Haunts of the South). I am sure the organ music is very relaxing to him after a long day watching over the gaol.

Another tale of paranormal activity at the church involve the ghost of Reverend Goodwin himself. His presence is sometimes seen by people at the church. Besides Goodwin's spirit and other activity inside of the church, the outside boasts frequent paranormal activity as well.

Bruton Parish Church houses the oldest graves in Colonial Williamsburg. Witnesses claim to have seen shadow figures of colonial era men which enter the cemetery and then disappear. There's also been another apparition spotted out here. This ghost has a long neck and is thought to be the spirit of a hanging victim.

Whether the spirits at Bruton Parish Church are related to its early Colonial Days (as may be the case with Peter Pelham) or its more modern 1900s incarnation, or both is still a mystery. The church is a wonderful slice of early Americana and a fabulous Historic Haunt. I hope to go back soon and listen for the ethereal organ music again.

# THE GHOSTS OF THE GOVERNOR'S PALACE

Governor's Palace, Colonial Williamsburg, VA

*The Governor's Palace*

Contractor Henry Cary began construction on the Governor's Palace in 1706. It was to be a two story brick home measuring 54 feet long and 48 feet wide with outbuildings; kitchen, stables, cellars, bath, and more. It consisted of 63 acres to the north of the Palace Green and wasn't finished until 1710. In the years to follow more buildings and gardens were added.

Alexander Spotswood, the first Governor, decorated the entrance hall with bayonet-tipped muskets. In 1714, it was called the palace for the first time. The Governors who lived in the Palace and proceded Spotswood were; Hugh Drysdale, William Gooch, Robert Dinwiddie, Francis Fauquier, Norborne Berkeley (Baron de Botetourt), John Murray (4th Earl of Dunmore), Patrick Henry, and Thomas Jefferson.

Over the years, each new Governor made additions or changes to the building. Many galas and grand parties were held here. It was also used as a hospital during the War of Independence.

On December 22nd, 1781 a fire, which was believed to have started in the basement, destroyed the building. The government sold the bricks off and the land was

# VIRGINIA
*Historic Haunts of the South III*

used for many things throughout the years until the Colonial Williamsburg Foundation got a hold of the property and reconstructed the grand Governor's Palace. The reconstructed palace opened April 23rd, 1934. It looks very much like it did when Governor Dunmore lived here.

## The Palace's Paranormal

There are many areas here at the Palace that are reported to be haunted or have had paranormal incidents. The maze area is said to be haunted by Civil War and Revolutionary War soldiers who are buried nearby on the property. These ghosts may account for much of the activity.

Some witnesses have reported seeing the apparition of a patient from Eastern State Mental Institute. The mental patient reportedly escaped in the 1920s and is said to have committed suicide. Several guests and staff members have seen a spirit walking the grounds wearing what appears to be a hospital gown.

Another apparition reported on the property has been named Elizabeth. She has been sighted on the Palace Grounds and the Palace Green. Some believe she is actually lady Anne Skipwith, who also haunted the Wythe House on the Green.

## My Thoughts on the Palace Haunts

With all the time I have spent at the Governor's Palace, I was surprised that it was one of the few Colonial Williamsburg places where I never felt much activity was present. In fact I really only felt anything active in the area of the maze and in the garden. I can't say that it was anything paranormal for sure, but I do not doubt the reports of the Palace and its grounds being haunted. There have been too many reports over the years and coincidences to doubt it.

# WASHINGTON'S LOOK-A-LIKE GHOST?
*Private Residence Colonial Williamsburg, VA*

This is a story about the house I lived in.

It was a reconstruction dated from 1940, but built using the old methods and it sits on the original 18th century foundation. It used to be an "ordinary" (similar to a coffee house). It was called "Burdett's Ordinary" in the 18th century. Some of our founding fathers visited this establishment, including: Patrick Henry, Thomas Jefferson, and George Washington.

Today it is one of the rare structures in the heart of Colonial Williamsburg that are used for private residences and not as old city buildings (like the tavern or the wig shop). I was fortunate to call this building home for a while during my time here in Williamsburg. I have a fondness for the place of course and more than a few ghost stories.

## Ghost Stories

At 3 am on Halloween night 2005, I was awoken by something. I had the feeling someone was watching me from the foot of the bed. I looked and saw a man who stood around 6 feet tall and was dressed in a dark brown colored colonial suit, with graying hair. I looked closer and soon realized this man strongly resembled George Washington! The next morning I got up and spoke with two friends and told them what I had seen.

I then began to research this interesting phenomenon and found out some very interesting facts. Indeed, Mr. Washington had visited the ordinary on numerous occassions while in Williamsburg. I also found a portrait of him in his inauguration suit and it looked exactly like the one I saw the apparition wearing.

Besides this unusual Washington "Look-a-like", we also often felt a presence in the house and heard footsteps. Everyone who visited me while I lived there said they felt a presence. Many times when I would be sitting downstairs in the study it would sound like someone was moving furniture upstairs. Or if I was upstairs it would sound as if it were downstairs.

Could what I have seen really have been the ghost of George Washington? Who knows?!?! The details of this Historic Haunt and private residence remain a mystery.

## VIRGINIA
*Historic Haunts of the South III*

# LAVENDER HEIGHTS POTENTIAL HAUNTS (AND AMAZING SHEETS)

*Lavender Heights Bed and Breakfast, Fredericksburg, Virginia*

*Lavender Heights B&B*

I love the smell of Lavender, its one of my favorite scents. Recently while researching this book we had the joy of staying in an amazing Bed and Breakfast surrounded with lavender scents and accents. Lavender Heights, Bed and Breakfast, in Fredericksburg Virginia. We came to Virginia to investigate reports of it being haunted, and were pleasantly surprised along the way.

### Lavender Heights Background and Paranormal Incidents

The original part of the bed and breakfast was built in the 1880s and is located on Forbes Street, formerly known as Telegraph Road. It was the main road in Fredericksburg. The inn is located on 6.7 acres of land that was tread upon by Union Forces during the Civil War. Captain Rufus T. Pettits' artillery battery was most likely based on the property according to old historical records from the Civil War era.

Despite contradictory historical reports, retired military member and owner of Lavender Heights, Jenny Holbert made a strong case that those accounts were incorrect and that according to overhead property maps, typographical maps and surveys Pettit's artillery force may have in fact been on the property of her now Bed and Breakfast. Pettit's desire for a position "that dominated the lower valley" and "drove every man on the field from their guns" would certainly be accomplished from this vantage point. The fact that Confederate Forces, under this multi-day artillery bombardment, "rallied and returned to their guns to return fire," would explain the number of Civil War era bullets and artillery fragments Jenny has discovered on site. It would also explain the possible reports of Civil War related paranormal activity.

### Lavender Heights Haunts

As previously mentioned Civil War spirits have been encountered on the property. This is no surprise in Fredericksburg with all the action its seen. However, the Lavender Height's position on the hill makes it more interesting.

Other reports of activity drew our interest. There are reports of a spirit animal on the grounds, believed to be a cat. The sounds of pitter patter of little paws and the ghostly sensation of something brushing up against your leg has been reported by guests. There is also supposedly a female spirit reported here who loves fresh flowers. The B&B's owner, Jenny Holbert, loves flowers herself and has planted them in several locations on the grounds. This seems to make the resident female spirit very happy.

When Holbert first moved into the inn, the former dining room was her bedroom (it is now a guest room). She was awoken one night by a ticking sound coming from the area that is now the sitting room of that suite. She got up from bed and explored the room. She couldn't find the sound or anything that could have been making it. As soon as she went back to bed, she heard it again.

Months later it became a guest suite. She had all but forgotten about the ticking she experienced until a guest staying in that suite reported an annoying ticking sound that woke him up. It seems someone was trying to get their attention.

## Historic Haunts Investigates

In June 2015 my husband Deric and I had the opportunity to investigate the inn for two nights to see what we might experience. We set up several cameras and digital recorders to see what evidence we might capture. We walked the entire property to get a base EMF and temperature reading of the premises. The EMF throughout the inn and property were between 0.0 and 0.8 except for one location near a heavy amount of wiring with fluctuations attributed to the interference. The temperature showed very little difference except near the family burial plot at the back of the property which read about 4 degrees cooler than anywhere else.

While we walked the property we did find an area where we believe a well once stood. By using dowsing rods we found a spot that would have been perfect for the water well. The rods crossed very strongly in that area.

While conducting an EVP session outside near the cemetery we did hear footsteps which sounded like three or four people were walking up the hill. I also clearly heard the sound of twigs snapping, but when I looked, there was no one to be found. Could this be spirits of Civil War soldiers heading to their posts or charging the hill?

During our research we were sitting in the dining room reviewing old newspaper articles, maps, records, etc. about the property and we actually got a very high EMF spike briefly when we first pulled all the paper work out. There were no nearby electronics or obvious explanations for it. It never repeated, however, and we chalked it up to an unusual incident.

After reviewing several hours of video and audio we unfortunately didn't capture anything paranormal on this investigation attempt. However, I did pick up something. It was a personal experience. A sensation that felt as though the lady of the house was welcoming us into her home. Perhaps this was the same woman who reportedly loved fresh flowers?

The inn is truly beautiful and definitely haunted with history and maybe a few spirits too. This is our favorite place to stay in Fredericksburg and Jenny was a fabulous host and cook. Also, just a heads up, the sheets in the guest rooms are absolutely amazing. I experienced the best night's sleep I've ever had on those Comphy Sheets!

# VIRGINIA
*Historic Haunts of the South III*

# WASHINGTON'S PROTECTIVE GHOST
*George Washington's Mount Vernon, Mount Vernon, Virginia*

George Washington, the " Father of our Country", was a remarkable man. His place in history and in the founding of our country is set, however, his spirit is apparently more mobile and has frequently been reported in various places at Mount Vernon, his old home.

Mount Vernon

### A Brief History of Washington

George Washington was born on February 22nd, 1732 at his parent's (Augustine and Mary Bell Washington) plantation on Popes Creek Estate in Westmoreland County Virginia. In 1735, the family, wealthy tobacco planters, moved to Little Hunting Creek Plantation (later named Mount Vernon). It was a small one and a half story farm house. In 1738, the family moved again to Ferry Farm near Fredericksburg. Washington would later inherit Ferry Farm and Mount Vernon.

Little is known about Washington's childhood, but many popular fables were written about him emphasizing his honesty, strength, and bravery. Two famous stories attributed to him were both invented, In the first he supposedly threw a silver dollar across the Potomac River (over a mile wide at Mt. Vernon), a herculean task which is impossible for a normal person. The second, and more well known, was the cherry tree story which was also invented (and perhaps intended to show the truthful nature of our first President).

Washington's father died when George was only 11 years old, he never attended college and his formal education actually ended when he was only 15 years of age. He didn't learn a foreign language like most colonial gentlemen did (many knew Latin and Greek). He became a surveyor thanks to his half-brother and surrogate father Lawrence at the age of 17. Through Lawrence he also acquired a military commission and at 21 in 1753, Governor Dinwiddie sent Washington to fight in the French and Indian War. By 1755 he became Lieutenant Colonel. In 1758, he resigned when peace was settled upon and he returned to Mount Vernon.

On January 6th, 1759, George married wealthy widow Martha Dandridge Custis who already had two children with her deceased husband (John Parker Custis and Martha Parke Custis). Washington farmed from 1759 to 1775 at Mount Vernon. During this time he doubled the size of Mount Vernon through land bounties and shrewd purchases . He also diversified his tobacco growing into other successful ventures and proved a capable businessman. He remained so until he became General of the Continental Army during the American Revolutionary War, a war for independence (June 1775-October 19th, 1781). General Cornwallis surrendered at the Battle of Yorktown, Virginia and Washington resigned from commission on December 23rd, 1783.

# VIRGINIA

*Washington's Protective Ghost*

In 1787 Washington presided over the Constitutional Convention and became the first President of the United States serving two terms from 1789-1793 and again from 1793-1797 (and initiating the term "Mr. President", when referring to our Commander in Chief). After the Presidency, he returned to Mount Vernon yet again, but in less than two years he became very ill after surveying property. On December 12th, 1799 he became bed ridden and could hardly move or care for himself. He told his wife Martha, upon his deathbed, to free his slaves and burn his personal documents. President Washington died on December 14th, 1799 in his bed chamber. Washington's funeral was held in the New Room of their home on December 18th, 1799 and he is entombed in their family tomb at Mount Vernon.

## More About Mt. Vernon

George Washington did not inherit the property right away upon his father's death. He leased it until 1763. However, he did expand the house in 1758 and added the cupola and the north and south wings in 1774. The property was named after Admiral Edward Vernon, Lawrence Washington's commanding officer in the War of Jenkins Ear in the 1740s. It is ten times the size of an average colonial home and is not symmetrical, but that is how Washington wanted it. Mt. Vernon was his own unique place and provided him with much happiness, so much so that his spirit was said to have come back.

## The Spirits of Mt. Vernon

Reports of the paranormal date back to the early 19th century. These really started right after Washington's death. Many claimed to have seen his apparition throughout the estate.

Some details of these paranormal incidents were reported by Josiah Quincy III. He arrived at Mount Vernon to meet with Washington's nephew, Bushrod Washington, and stayed overnight. Quincy reported that while sleeping that night in Washington's former bed chamber, he spied the deceased President's apparition.

Many others have reported seeing his apparition and feeling his presence. It has been suggested that in some case he appears to those who callously handle or mistreat his place or his belongings. Others have reported feeling ill within his bedroom. Voices and footsteps have also been heard throughout his home.

## My Own Experiences

I had my own personal experiences at Mt. Vernon when I visited here in 2010 with Mikey Pfeifer, a member of my Historic Haunts team and a good friend. I knew very little about the layout of the home but while on the 2nd floor I approached one of the bedrooms and looking into the room stated "Washington died here." I also felt very ill while in and near his bedroom until I went down the hallway.

Another area where there was a very strong presence was standing at Washington's tomb. We definitely were not alone while there paying our respects. If you are a fan of American history, this is a location that you truly have to see and experience for yourself and is another on top of our Historic Haunts list.

## VIRGINIA
*Historic Haunts of the South III*

# THE POE-TENTIAL GHOST OF A MASTER OF THE MACABRE
*Edgar Allan Poe Museum, Richmond, Virginia*

*Poe Museum in the "Old Stone House"*

Edgar Allan Poe is one of my writing heroes! He is definitely an influence in my decision to write about the paranormal. Poe is credited with creating or mastering the short story, detective fiction, science fiction, lyric poetry and of course the horror story. He has even been called "America's Shakespeare". To some at the Poe Museum in Richmond, he's also a frequent ghostly visitor.

**Poe's Past and the Old Stone House**

Edgar Poe was born on January 19th, 1809 in Boston Massachusetts. After Poe's father abandoned the family in 1910 and his mother passed the following year, Poe was left a young orphan. He was taken in by John and Frances Allen of Richmond, Virginia, but despite adding the Allen to his name was never formally adopted. He was with the couple in Virginia well into his young adulthood.

Well before he was born the building that housed The Poe Museum in Richmond was constructed in 1740 by Jacob Ege, a German immigrant. Ege moved to Philadelphia in 1738 before later relocating to Richmond. He originally built the home for himself and his new wife Maria Dorothea Scheerer.

Additions were made to the home in 1754. Ege died a short time later in 1762. His son Samuel owned the home after Jacob's death until he too died and passed it on. Coincidentally, at the age of 15, Edgar Allan Poe was a rifleman, part of a volunteer company of young Richmonders called the Junior Morgan Rifleman, and stood as honor guard of the house while the Marquis de Lafayette revisited here in 1824. The house remained in the Ege family until 1911.

In the middle of Poe's centennial in 1909 there was a strong push by a group of Richmond residents for the city to better recognize one of its most famous residents. The city blocked the group's efforts to build a statue of Poe on Monument Avenue. So the Preservation Virginia Group saved the old house with a connection to Poe and decided to open the museum.

The aptly named "Old Stone House" is the oldest original building in Richmond and was mere blocks away from Poe's first home with the Allans and from his first place of employment, the Southern Literary Messenger. Poe never actually lived in the home, but this museum now houses the largest collection of Poe's work, first editions, memorabilia, relics, letters, and more. The museum opened in 1922 as a lasting tribute to the great author. It also contains a unique look at 19th century Richmond with an overview of what it was like to live there during Poe's time.

## The Spirits of the Museum

There have been literally hundreds of reports of paranormal activity at the museum, including footsteps, orbs, and other unusual phenomenon. One of the more interesting is that of the ghostly children. A pair of blonde-haired children believed to be members of the Ege family have not appeared in ghostly form to guests in the building, but they have appeared with remarkable frequency in photographs taken in the building. These spirits often "photo-bomb" photographs taken by museum visitors appearing after the picture is captured or the film developed. In fact, this phenomenon has been happening for twenty years! In all that time the children never seem to age and have often appeared with another resident spirit, a shadowy figure many think to be well known.

Besides the children's spirits, a shadowy ghost has been encountered at Poe's museum and while some speculate this could be Jacob Ege haunting the property, most believe that it is in fact the ghost of Poe himself who still haunts this building. Since there are so many personal items that once belonged to him, it would be no small wonder that he would haunt here from time to time. It could very well be a strong case of spirit attachment.

Indeed the shadowy figure has been seen wandering the halls and seems particularly drawn to a hand mirror owned by Poe's beloved wife Virginia, and a walking stick that he left in Richmond. The shadowy figure has been seen in the building and in the garden where a Poe shrine had been erected from salvaged bricks of Poe's former employer the Southern Literary Messenger.

One other occurrence of note humorously enough involved Poe's "bobble-heads". A shipment of these items was reportedly mysteriously unpacked and lined up by a pair of unseen hands. Even more amazing is that this was accomplished without setting off the museum's sensitive motion and other alarms.

## Historic Haunts Investigates

On a visit here in 2010 with my dear friend and Historic Haunts team member Mike Pfeifer, we explored the museum and the property. We didn't come into contact with Mr. Poe's spirit (which would have been an honor for me) and we didn't hear the footsteps, but at certain locations and near certain artifacts I did feel a presence. This was of course in the areas where Poe's personal items were incased. Mike on the other hand felt a strong sense of sadness in different sections of the museum.

Whether Poe's spirit is here or not, the museum is haunted with amazing pieces of literary history and shouldn't be missed if you find yourself in Richmond. To me, Poe is the King of macabre. To others he's the inspiration for literary giants and quite a few literary Historic Haunts.

Also, while you are in Richmond, pay your respects to Poe's birth mother Eliza. She is buried in St. John's Episcopal Church. This is also a great stop on a tour of Patrick Henry's historic hot spots.

# ABOUT THE AUTHOR
## *Jamie Roush Pearce*

Jamie Pearce lives in the Jacksonville, Florida area with her husband Deric and their cat Griffon. With over 20 years of experience in the paranormal field and five books under her belt, Jamie Pearce is obviously a fan of the paranormal.

However, she has a passion for more than history and the paranormal, she is also a scuba diver and avid runner. As a child she wanted to be a marine biologist and a fitness trainer. Even though her career path went in a different direction, she still has a passion for the ocean and being fit.

Another passion of hers is traveling and she has many new locations in mind for the future that she and her husband will hopefully be visiting. Ideally they will be featured in upcoming books. Pearce currently has four more books in the Historic Haunts series in progress and is always looking for new and exciting haunted locations. She continues to post the evidence of her investigations and research of the paranormal through her website **www.historic-haunts.net** and with her team **Historic Haunts Investigations. She can also be connected to on Facebook:** www.facebook.com/HistoricHaunts
www.facebook.com/AuthorJamiePearce

Use the following pages to log your own paranormal experiences at the locations in the book or at others:

Made in the
USA
Columbia, SC

81936022R10065